THE GREEN G

Here's Health

THE GREEN GUIDE

Angela Smyth & Caroline Wheater

ARGUS BOOKS

Argus Books
Argus House
Boundary Way
Hemel Hempstead
Hertfordshire HP2 7ST
England

First published by Argus Books 1990

ISBN 1 85486 005 4

Phototypesetting by ''The Works'', Exeter, Devon
Printed and bound in England by Richard Clay Ltd., Bungay, Suffolk

Contents

Introduction

For many years *Here's Health* has talked of the link between a healthy body and a healthy environment. The magazine's philosophy has always been to promote a chemical-free existence, pure food, water and air, and to warn its readers of the fact that a polluted world will inevitably lead to ill health.

Now the rest of the world is also talking about it. Green issues have reached the top of political agendas, accompanied by an explosion of media coverage. Environmental groups which for years were considered cranks and extremists are now seeing their memberships soaring by the thousands.

This book is published at a time when green issues are at the forefront of political campaigning. The Green Party saw a surge in popularity in the 1989 European elections, proving the public's concern for the environment. Green concepts are no longer limited to the cranks but are now increasingly seen as the responsibility of society at large.

Few today can escape the concern generated for the environment. CFCs in aerosols, nitrates in water, and pesticides in food have become household issues. Public awareness is reflected in the epidemic of 'environmentally friendly' labels, the boom in bottled water sales and the militancy of parents campaigning for safe food and unpolluted air. But coverage of these issues is fragmented by media sensationalism and the reluctance of governments to finance necessary changes. Often the public does not get the full story. CFCs are nasties which destroy the ozone layer — we can't see them, what are they? The ozone layer is up there, we're down here, so how can a squirt of hair-spray destroy the earth's protective shield?

The aim of this book is to explain the principal environmental concerns of this century, since it is only by understanding how these operate that we can work to avert them. It is not enough to leave such issues to the control of governments. When the environment is threatened, urgent action is needed and governments have a habit of putting things off until the last minute. For many years environmentalists and scientists have been telling us that our water is unsafe, the greenhouse effect is encroaching and acid rain is accumulating, but moves for change have not yet happened.

There is no doubt that legislation on a national or international level has its impact: the claims by state leaders saying CFCs must go have resulted in manufacturers finding ways of producing environmentally friendly alternatives. After a long struggle and pressure by campaigning groups, EEC legislation has pushed European governments to clean up their water. But such action takes time, and it is not until public concern is at its height that change is initiated. So it is the public which ultimately holds the reins of environmental protection.

What is happening to our planet is not just a chance of fate, it is the result of the way we live. As we wrote this book the same theme appeared in every chapter: the environmental disaster facing us is a result of pure and indiscriminate over-consumption of resources.

It may be a desire to buy a new car every two years, or maybe to invest in a new mahogany fitted kitchen. Or perhaps the accumulation of synthetic plastics or exotic pets from far-flung climes. What we buy and how much we consume has a major impact on the environment we live in. Even an action as simple as buying a tin of tuna fish affects the planet in its own small way.

Consumerism has boomed in the last 20 years and it is probably here to stay. In this book we are not advocating a 'sack and sandal' approach to life, but a move away from products which harm the environment to ones which sustain it, a move towards quality, not quantity, and a move to invest in products which last, not short-life items which are discarded and left to clutter our habitat. The nations of the world should now be thinking in terms of sustainable development, that is development which meets the needs of the present without compromising the ability of future generations to meet their own needs.

Our technological knowledge and skills make it possible to find solutions to the problems facing the planet. It is not a question of going backwards, but moving forwards to produce or adapt consumer goods so that they are not destructive. The process has already begun with the invention of clean energy technologies, environmentally friendly washing machines and dishwashers, and cars adapted to run on unleaded petrol. It is up to the consumer to be aware of these alternatives and encourage them.

It is easy to make the changes when alternatives are laid on. What is more difficult is to break habits and ideas: a consumer policy of 'what I want and what is fashionable' will have to change to 'what I need and what is sustainably available'. It means, perhaps, making the decision to eat less meat and buy fewer processed foods; it means insulating the loft to preserve energy; and it means making a trip to the bottle bank with the empties.

To live in an environmentally friendly way is not difficult, but it requires time and effort which few of us are prepared to give. It is up to those in power to ensure that green options are easy and cheap options. We have seen the effects of the Government's support for unleaded petrol, now available nationwide at a lower price than leaded. A similar scheme to encourage paper, glass and metal recycling would considerably ease the burden of waste disposal. Such policies come only as a result of public pressure, and, as the political parties compete to be greenest, it is essential that the voting public understands the issues at stake and what must be done to protect the environment.

Governments can make mistakes. Financial incentives can be put before environmental concerns. For this reason, there is also an essential role for non-political, independent organisations to monitor and control what is happening to the environment, both at home and abroad, and to campaign for change where necessary. It is the research of these organisations which, over the years, has brought green issues to the front pages of national newspapers. By joining such organisations, your support will allow them to continue to protect our planet.

Chapter 1

The Greenhouse Effect

In the last ten years our planet has seen a series of disasters and freak weather patterns. Scenes of starving, drought-ridden Africa, the flooded streets of Bangladesh, the parched wheat plains of America's Mid West, typhoons in the Philippines and frozen noses in Alaska are familiar to our TV screens. Even Europe has felt the change: in 1989 we saw the worst skiing season for 20 years and a steaming hot summer which will go down in history.

All over the world the rumour spreads that we are heading for an environmental disaster. Governments are holding conferences to discuss with trepidation what is happening to the world's weather. The earth is heating up, they say, it's called the 'greenhouse effect'. What does it mean? When we have a decent summer does it signify a climatic disaster?

No one is exactly sure what is causing the climatic variations and extremes seen over the last ten years. There are a number of factors which influence climate: external influences such as the extent of the sun's output or a change in the degree of explosive volcanic activity, or internal mechanisms such as a shift in the ocean temperature distribution. It has also been known for 100 years that the atmospheric gases surrounding the planet play an important role in determining its temperature and climatic variability.

In the 1820s a French mathematician, Baron Jean Baptiste Fourier, came up with the theory that the earth's atmosphere acts like the transparent glass cover of a box. Just like the windows of a greenhouse, the gases forming the atmosphere of the planet allow the sun's heat and light to radiate through them, but do not allow all the warmth that radiates back from the earth to pass out into space. The result is that a certain amount of heat is trapped between the earth's surface and the earth's atmospheric barrier, keeping the planet at just the right temperature to sustain life.

Once upon a time, the planet's atmosphere was a delicate combination of carbon dioxide, water and small quantities of methane — natural substances brought up from the interior of the planet by volcanoes. This balance of gases provided a protective blanket shrouding the earth and holding in just the right amount of heat. Without these gases the earth would have frozen solid.

That was in the beginning. Since the onset of the Industrial Revolution, we have pumped out 25 per cent more carbon dioxide into the atmosphere. The world's protective blanket has been thickened by more carbon dioxide, along with vast quantities of other naturally formed gases and industrial by-products. The thicker the blanket becomes, the more heat it traps. The more heat that is trapped, the warmer the earth becomes.

Climatologists today believe that the changes in weather which have been experienced over the last ten years may be due both to natural climatic variability and to an underlying warming trend caused by a thickening of the earth's atmospheric blanket, otherwise known as the 'greenhouse effect'. Scientists say that conclusive evidence to establish the link beyond reasonable doubt will only occur when the earth gets hotter than it would during natural changes in climate. This should happen within the next 25 years. But to wait for conclusive evidence would allow the greenhouse effect to continue for too long, and could be fatal.

> *Humanity is conducting an uncontrolled globally pervasive experiment whose ultimate consequences could be second only to global nuclear war.*
> The Changing Atmosphere: Implications for Global Security, Toronto, June, 1988.

Global warming

Almost a century ago, scientists were aware of the fact that, by burning coal, we were releasing into the atmosphere a wall of carbon dioxide gas which could result in a warming of the planet. Now climatologists have evidence to confirm that this is happening. Computer models of climatic systems show that the planet has gradually warmed over the last century. This warmth is now increasing at an unprecedented rate. Overall, since the mid 1980s, the earth has warmed by more than 0.5°C, breaking the record for the warmest year in 1980, 1981, 1983, and 1987. Scientists at the Institute of Climatic Research at the University of East Anglia expect temperatures to increase by up to 4.5°C in the next 50 years. Such small temperature variations may seem insignificant, until we compare them to former fluctuations in global temperatures. A drop of 4°C would take us back to conditions of the last Ice Age. A rise of 4°C would make the earth hotter than it has been for 100,000 years, says the Institute.

Research on earth is backed up by examination of the climate on other planets. Venus, for example, has a dense fog of carbon dioxide surrounding it, making its temperature intolerably hot. Mars, on the other hand, has a fragile layer of carbon dioxide, which does not trap enough heat to support life. What makes our planet the perfect temperature for life is the delicate exchange of gases between the earth and the atmosphere.

This delicate combination of gases is maintained in balance by the carbon cycle. Carbon is stored in the oceans, fossil fuels, sedimentary rocks, living plants and animals as well as in the atmosphere. It is continuously transferred between these different sources, entering and leaving as required. If, however, too much carbon is put into the atmosphere faster than it can be removed, an imbalance occurs.

The causes

Industrialisation has brought about the mining and burning of vast quantities of fossil fuels: coal, gas and oil. With it has come a growth in population. To accommodate and feed the ever growing numbers, forests and plant life have been cleared for housing and intensive agriculture. When trees are felled or burnt, carbon dioxide is released into the atmosphere. With fewer trees and plants, less carbon dioxide is removed from the atmosphere. Deforestation and changing land use have made a major contribution to the historical rise in carbon dioxide levels.

Estimated Breakdown Of CO_2 Emissions in the UK (1987)

Emissions by Fuel Type

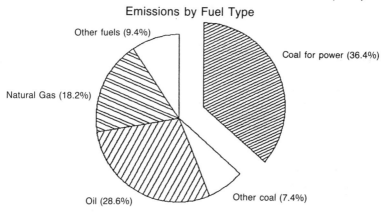

Emissions by Sector

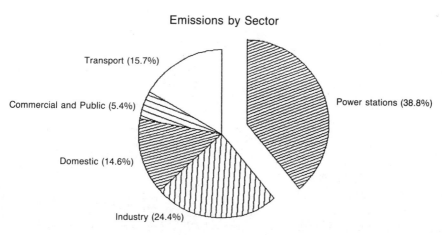

Source: Friends of the Earth.

But carbon dioxide is not the only greenhouse culprit. With the rise in population, the atmospheric content of methane, another globe warming gas, has risen to contribute to the ever-thickening global blanket. Methane concentrations have doubled over the past 200 years. The gas is produced when organic carbon compounds break down in waterlogged soils, such as rice paddy fields. Methane is also a by-product of rotting waste buried in the soil. Cattle farming also contributes to the levels emitted — methane results from digestion.

From the exhausts of our cars and the chimneys of our power stations, nitrous oxide, another greenhouse gas, is pumped into the atmosphere. Even in the countryside, the use of fertilisers on the soil encourages the accumulation of this gas which hangs around in the atmosphere for almost two centuries. With it comes the hazy smog-like apparition over cities — tropospheric ozone — yet another global warmer, created when sunlight reacts with car and power station emissions. Two more layers are thus added to the earth's protective blanket.

Technological invention has brought us chlorofluorocarbons (CFCs), the chemicals used to propel air sprays out of aerosol cans and to keep fridges and air conditioning systems cool. Industry has seen a boom in their production since the 1970s. CFCs are the most powerful of the planet's warmers: one molecule is 10,000 times more effective at trapping heat than one carbon dioxide molecule. They are particularly insidious, since there are few natural mechanisms for their removal in the lower atmosphere, and consequently they hang around with us for up to 100 years and are broken down only under the influence of ultraviolet light in the upper atmosphere. There they create a doubly damaging effect by nibbling a hole in the ozone layer, the world's vital protection from radiation.

Principal pollutants involved in the problems of photochemical smog and acid rain, ozone depletion and greenhouse warming.

Source: Karas, J. H. W. and Kelly, P. M. Global implications of air pollution. In: *Proceedings, SAM and APPEN International Conference on Global Development and Environment Crisis*, Penang, Malaysia, 1987.

As the combination of these powerful gases increases, so the planetary blanket thickens and the earth below becomes hot, sticky and irritable. Climatologists predict that the climatic changes which will result will bring disaster to human activity and lifestyle, agriculture, availability of food and the management of nature's systems.

> *The changes which will occur in the future will be without precedent in mankind's experience. Unless we find a solution to the greenhouse effect we will be faced with serious irreversible damage to the environment.*
> Climatic Research Unit, University of East Anglia, 1989.

The consequences

For some years now, the UK has undertaken a number of research studies looking into the potential effects of the greenhouse effect. Results of the research show that the most obvious impact of global warming will be felt in coastal and river areas as the sea levels rise. As the earth's temperatures increase, the glaciers will melt, pouring a greater volume of water through the world's deltas. A higher global temperature will also cause the oceans to expand and rise in level. Cities, agricultural land, water sources, beaches and coastal wetlands will be at risk of inundation or storm-induced flooding.

Flooded fields in Lincolnshire. Low lying land near the coast is vulnerable to flooding.

All countries will feel the effects, although the impact will undoubtedly be greater in low-lying land and the communities living in coastal regions — estimated at 3 billion people. The communities of major concern are those living on the unprotected Nile delta of Egypt and the Ganges delta of Bangladesh. It is forecast that a rise in the level of the Nile of only 50cm would render homeless nearly 16 per cent of Egypt's population. A 2m rise in the level of the Ganges would wash away the homes of 27 per cent of the people of Bangladesh.

> *Change is at present taking place at a rate some ten times faster than the average over the last 10,000 years... Nearly half of humanity lives within 60 kilometres of a coastline. A rise in mean sea level of only 25cm would have substantial effects.*
> Sir Crispin Tickell, Britain's Ambassador to the United Nations, June 1989.

It is not only the Third World which would be affected by rising sea levels. Cities with buildings bordering onto an eroding coastline — skyscrapers in New York and Rio de Janiero, for example — would also be vulnerable. The Netherlands has experience of the effects of flooding from the North Sea — farmland ruined by sand and salt takes years to regain its fertility. Nearer to home, Britain's east coast is predicted to be highly susceptible to flooding, as are large areas of Norfolk. The price of improving sea defences to avoid the impact of rising sea in Britain alone is estimated to run to between £5 and £8 billion.

Changing patterns of global carbon dioxide emissions.

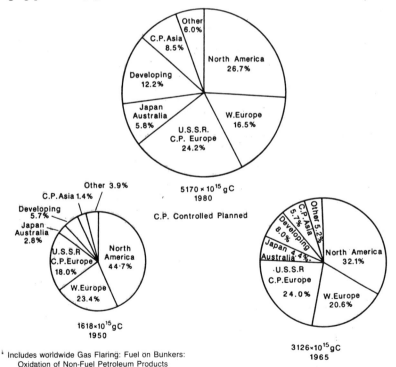

ⁱ Includes worldwide Gas Flaring: Fuel on Bunkers: Oxidation of Non-Fuel Petroleum Products

Source: Rotty, R.M. and Masters, C. *Past and Future Releases of CO2 from Fossil Fuel Combustion.* Institute for Energy Analysis, Oak Ridge, 1984.

   The greenhouse effect would bring flooding on the one hand, drought on the other. Another major implication of global warming would be its effect on agriculture. Researchers say that increases of carbon dioxide levels, climatic change and a rise in sea levels would all directly affect food availability. To begin with, high levels of carbon dioxide may directly increase the growth and yield of major food crops; however, it will also be favourable to the proliferation of weeds and pests which could become a serious problem. Water availability will also be disrupted. Today, crops are selected and grown to take best advantage of a particular temperature and rainfall regime — they are often unable to stand up to climatic changes or extremes. Over the last two years there has been a serious drying out of the continental interiors of North America and the USSR, areas which are particularly sensitive to changes in moisture availability. Great grain plains, such as these, could see a decrease in yield of up to 17 per cent if the earth's heat rises by 2°C. The 1989 drought in the US Mid West vividly demonstrated the impact: grain output was down by 31 per cent, leaving the world grain stocks depleted by 38 per cent. The USA provides 90 per cent of the world's grain surplus. This bread basket, which supports the rest of the world when its harvests fail, could soon be empty.

Soil erosion in North Tanzania after clearance of forest.

   It is not just areas of temperate latitude whose agriculture will be affected. Over most of the subtropics and tropics, food production is critically dependent on the timing, reliability and quantity of rainfall. Climatologists forecast that the changes in the monsoon rain resulting from global warming will have a major impact on the production of rice. This crop, which provides staple food for 60 per cent of the world's population, is particularly sensitive to climatic changes. Failure of its harvest could have devastating results on food availability in the Third World.

Flooding and drought are severe problems in themselves. With them come thousands of destroyed homes and hungry refugees. Such migration could lead to the disruption of entire continents, terrorism, civil wars and ultimately economic breakdown. This fact was emphasised in 1989 by Sir Crispin Tickell, Britain's ambassador to the United Nations and the British Government's most senior adviser on global warming, in a speech given to the Natural Environment Research Council, when he said:

> 'Even if only 1 per cent (a very low estimate) of a world population of six billion were affected by the effects of global warming, that would mean some 60 million environmental refugees. The world has never had to cope with such numbers of homeless and desperate people.'

In areas which are not hit by flooding and famine disasters, the effects of global warming will be felt, albeit to a lesser degree. Climatic changes will bring the failure of reservoir and water systems, affecting both water availability and quality. Increased heat in some areas may cause health problems, particularly in the elderly. Warmer climes favour the transmission of certain diseases and parasites. The economy could also be struck, particularly in coastal areas dependent on dockland industry or water-related activities and tourism.

Britain's fate

In 1987 the Department of the Environment commissioned a series of study reports from independent consultants in universities and research institutes on the impact of the greenhouse effect on the UK. The results of these studies were based on predictions that, by the year 2050, carbon dioxide levels could be twice as high as those found in pre-industrial Britain. Under these circumstances, the UK will experience a rise in average temperature of 3°C, a 20 per cent change in average rainfall of almost one metre.

Information gained at UK workshops and international meetings concluded that the climate of southern Britain will become closer to that of south west-France (warm and humid). Southern, central and eastern England will become drier and semi-Mediterranean in climate, while northern England and Scotland will become warmer and more temperate but not necessarily drier. On the whole, says the report, the country will experience warmer and wetter winters with drier and warmer summers.

A rise in sea level of between 29cm and 165cm is expected in Britain, putting at risk areas around the estuaries of the Thames, the Humber, the Tees, the Forth, the Tay, the Ribble, the Mersey and the Bristol Channel and the low-lying coasts in Kent, Essex, East Anglia and Lancashire. Loss of land will affect industry, tourism and wildlife. The coast most at risk from rising sea levels includes the marshes and mud flats which presently accommodate hundreds of thousands of native and migrant birds who will have nowhere to go.

Whatever the temperature and state of the land, researchers are in no doubt that global warming will bring more extreme climatic variability in Britain. This will not come without cost to the country's economy. A study by the Atmospheric Impacts Research Group at Birmingham University showed that the annual value of British agriculture can vary by up to one-third as a result of the weather. In property damages, climatic variations can cost insurance companies around £800 million a year in damages.

What can be done?

The greenhouse effect is not a theory confined to scientists' research laboratories. It has become a worldwide reality discussed at governmental level. In 1988, world leaders publicly acknowledged that human abuse had overstepped the mark and could no longer be ignored. At the Toronto Conference in June that year, 300 experts from 48 different countries concluded that cuts in carbon dioxide greater than 50 per cent will be needed to stabilise the climate, with 20 per cent cuts from 1988 levels by the year 2005 as 'an initial global goal'. The Hamburg Congress in the same year called for a 30 per cent reduction from major 'wealthy carbon dioxide producing nations' by the year 2000. These reductions are needed to keep temperature increases down to 0.1°C per decade. Without them, said the experts, warming could increase to 1°C per decade.

It has been accepted internationally that the first line of attack must be to reduce greenhouse gas emissions. Since no one activity contributes a dominant proportion of total emissions, this means reducing the emissions of all harmful gases through a concerted international effort. The most direct route to controlling greenhouse gas emissions is through reduction in energy consumption and increase in energy efficiency. The dilemma for the industrialised nations posed by this prospect is, in a society where 90 per cent of commercial global energy production is met by fossil fuel combustion, how can emissions be reduced without a dramatic fall in economy and lifestyle? The United Nations Environmental Programme claims that significant reductions in emissions are possible without a drop in living standards. Significant savings have already been made in the USA, Sweden and Norway by investment in sophisticated insulation and space heating systems, and the World Resources Institute claims that, by maximising use of existing energy saving technology and with limited development of new techniques, global energy consumption in 2020 need only be slightly higher than it is today.

Energy strategies will, however, have to change to bring down present levels of emissions. Firstly, nations will be encouraged to use oil and gas fuels rather than coal. Then there is potential for reducing fossil fuels altogether, by substituting with alternative energy sources such as solar, hydroelectric, wind, and wave power which could, say some sources, supply 50 to 70 per cent of global energy needs (see Chapter 2). Tax incentives and the imposition of environmental penalties for the use of polluting gases may also prove a fruitful means of shifting power production away from fossil fuels.

The reduction of emissions of other harmful greenhouse gases is already underway in some countries. The use of CFCs in aerosols was banned in the USA some years ago. As a result of consumer pressure, most manufacturers in the UK now produce aerosols which are free of CFCs, although they are still used in refrigerants and other industrial applications.

Methane and nitrous oxides are more difficult to eradicate, as their emissions are closely linked to population growth and food production. In the UK, a trend is developing to encourage a reduction in fertiliser use. Meanwhile the technology to clean up the exhausts of cars, available in the form of catalytic converters and enforced by law in the USA for some 15 years, is slow to be taken up in Europe.

While proposals are being made to reduce emissions and adopt new energy sources, concern over emission levels has provided a unique opportunity for the nuclear industry to advocate itself as the only 'clean' alternative. The Thatcher Government subsequently suggested that a massive expansion in nuclear capacity could, by itself, substantially reduce carbon dioxide emissions. However, a number of scientific studies have disputed this claim. One by the US Rocky Mountain Institute set out to establish how many nuclear reactors would be required to displace coal entirely as an energy source over the next few decades. Their results showed that, even if we were to construct a nuclear plant every three days at a cost of £80 billion per year over 37 years, we would still fail to reduce carbon dioxide emissions or the rate of global warming significantly. The study pointed out that, in any case, Third World countries would be unable to afford such investment in nuclear energy and that a scheme of energy conservation would be far more economically viable for all nations. The report claims that 'In the US, improving electrical efficiency is nearly seven times more cost effective than nuclear power for abating carbon dioxide emissions'.

Some researchers have made claims that nuclear expansion, combined with a programme of energy conservation, could be the solution to the greenhouse effect. Jose Goldemburg, a Brazilian economist, in a scenario called 'Energy for a Sustainable World', suggests that, if global energy consumption can be kept to a mere 10 per cent increase by the year 2020, a six-fold increase in nuclear capacity along with other 'clean' technologies could cut carbon dioxide emissions by 38 per cent.

But even this solution does not come cheap: a six-fold increase in nuclear expansion would cost around $1.8 trillion. Neither does it dismiss the problems, as yet unresolved, which the adoption of nuclear power brings — the hazards of catastrophic accidents, the management of radioactive waste and the risk of a proliferation of nuclear weapons. Apart from the nuclear option being an extremely expensive route to take to avert the greenhouse effect, it could also substitute one environmental disaster for another. In

1987, the World Commission on Environment and Development produced 'The Brundtland Report', which outlined the evidence available and the solutions proposed throughout the world for energy problems. The report concluded that:

> 'The generation of nuclear power is only justifiable if there are solid solutions to the presently unsolved problems to which it gives rise.'

Reports have been produced by environmentalists and scientists, by politicians and international delegates. The conclusions are all the same: the earth is warming, something must be done about it and fast. The top three priorities proposed are:

★ to introduce national and international programmes on energy conservation to reduce fossil fuel combustion

★ to phase out by 1995 CFCs and other substances which deplete the ozone layer

★ to reverse the current level of deforestation through the protection of rain forests and large tree planting programmes

Environmentalists are presently pressurising the British government to:

★ insist that the Electricity Supply Industry compares the cost of new supply investment with the cost of electricity conservation programmes and adopts the 'least cost' option, as is done in the USA.

★ encourage greater consumer choice in energy efficiency by introducing the labelling of electrical and gas appliances, heating and lighting systems in building and fuel efficiency in cars. Labelling should include 'pollution cost' information as well as running costs.

★ introduce grants and fiscal incentives for the improvement of energy efficiency in all sectors.

★ develop efficient public transport systems and encourage their use through fare subsidies and business taxes.

Take Action

While the impetus must come on a governmental level, there are also opportunities and a necessity for every individual to counteract global warming by personal action. This is how you can act now to halt global warming.

To save energy
— insulate your loft, walls and water tank
— use thermo-static valves on radiators to allow you to adjust the temperature in each room
— use environmentally friendly light bulbs and appliances (see Chapter 13)
— fit a gas condensing boiler
— switch off lights when not needed

To save forests
— avoid all products made from tropical hardwoods but if you have to buy them look for the Good Wood Seal of Approval (see Chapter 6)

— do not buy products which are over-packaged
— opt for recycled paper products

To save fuel
— use public transport or a bicycle
— only use a car when absolutely necessary
— share lifts if possible
— use a car which is low on petrol consumption, takes unleaded and has a catalytic converter
— help campaign for a better public transport system.

Chapter 2

Energy

Four thousand million years ago the sun, a burning ball of nuclear energy, exploded. One of the spinning fragments that shot into space was the earth. Enveloped by a cloud of gases with little or no oxygen, the sun's ultraviolet rays scorched down onto the earth's volatile surface. The seas were hot, volcanoes spouted ash and lava, and electrical storms crackled across the skies. From this immense cauldron of energy came the beginnings of life.

The sun's energy beams down on us still, sustaining us on a growing, breathing planet. Directly and indirectly, the sun provides all our specific energy needs, winds, waves, tides, solar power and firewood. It also acted as the catalyst to form fossil fuels from tiny animals millions of years ago. In the UK, 93 per cent of our energy comes from fossil fuels, oil (35.2 per cent), coal (32.2 per cent) and natural gas (25.2 per cent). We use it for heating, appliances, lighting, transport, electricity and industrial processes. On a global scale, 77 per cent of primary energy is created from fossil fuels, but these resources won't last forever. The human race is eating them up at a staggering rate.

Proportion of fuels used for primary energy worldwide

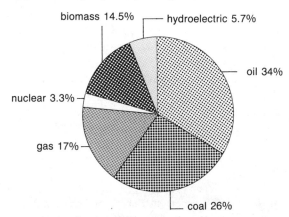

Source: Energy Without End, Friends of the Earth

Available UK coal stocks may last another three to four hundred years, North Sea gas used at current levels another 30 years, and we have already used over 40 per cent of North Sea oil. As fossil fuels become more difficult to recover from the earth's crust, and supplies diminish, prices will shoot sky high, just as they did in the oil crisis of 1973.

Another major threat that has arisen from the unrelenting use of fossil fuels is the steady build-up of carbon dioxide in the atmosphere which adds to the greenhouse effect (see Chapter 1). Carbon dioxide accounts for half of the greenhouse gases and, in global terms, 75 per cent of emissions comes from the burning of fossil fuels for energy.

The Association for the Conservation of Power estimates that carbon dioxide emissions could increase by up to 20 per cent in the year 2005 if the Government does not confront the problem. Alternatively, with a policy of energy efficiency and the adoption of renewable methods of energy generation, UK emissions could be slashed by 23 per cent in the same time.

Answers to increased demand

The fact is that demand for energy will probably continue to rise substantially. The Central Electricity Generating Board suggests an increased electricity demand of 20 per cent in Britain by the year 2000. Some global scenarios predict an increase of between 210 to 360 per cent by 2020, because of a larger world population and the needs of developing countries. The earth cannot continue to sustain such large drains on its environmental capital, or combat the greenhouse effect, unless major changes take place. The answer is simple — make energy efficiency a number one global priority and speed up the development of renewable energy technologies. For centuries we have taken unremittingly from the earth. Now, remaining supplies of fossil fuels should be saved, not squandered.

Energy efficiency and renewable energy go hand in hand. In 1987 the influential Brundtland Report, under the auspices of the World Commission on Environment and Development, stated that in order to meet world energy demand, more efficient use of resources was vital. Gro Harlem Brundtland, chairwoman and Prime Minster of Norway, said: 'We must be prepared to tackle the myth that energy consumption must be allowed to grow unchecked.' Tough standards of energy efficiency are perfectly possible to introduce, together with a combination of power from wind, solar, hydro, biofuels, and geothermal (heat from rocks) sources.

How energy is measured		
One watt	=	1 joule per second
One kilowatt (KW)	=	1000 watts
One megawatt (MW)	=	1000 kilowatts
One gigawatt (GW)	=	1000 megawatts
One terrawatt (TW)	=	1000 gigawatts

*One kilowatt hour (kWh) is equivalent to 1000 watts being used for one hour, or 2000 watts used for half an hour, or 100 watts used for ten hours.

British energy studies estimate that total energy consumption could be reduced by anything between 10 and 65 per cent over the next 35 years — depending on the political will. They have also shown that 60 per cent of the energy released from fossil fuels is wasted. Thirty per cent dissipates when the original fuel is converted into usable electricity, gas, petrol or solid fuels; and another 30 per cent vanishes into thin air because of inefficient systems and appliances in homes, industry and transport.

In a recent report by Friends of the Earth (FoE) to the House of Lords it was stated that Britain could reduce electricity demand by 70 per cent, just through energy efficiency. The report explains 'It would cost five to ten times less than building conventional power stations to meet demand, and it would have a significantly lower environmental impact'. So far, the energy efficiency option has not been seriously considered by the Government — Britain's energy policy relies on new sources of energy to meet demand.

Electricity

Although electricity only supplies 15 per cent of the UK's energy demand, it consumes almost a third of primary energy from fossil fuels. The guzzling of our resources is even more worrying when one realises that two-thirds of the energy produced in a power station floats straight out of the cooling towers, never to be seen again. This system is highly wasteful and could be made 80 per cent efficient if combined heat and power (CHP) technologies were installed. In CHP schemes, while the power station produces electricity, the waste hot steam is piped to local communities to meet heating demands. The underground system of pipes would service industry first, providing boiling hot steam, and then domestic homes that require lower temperature heat.

There are already several thousand CHP plants in the UK providing 15 per cent of electricity to industry, but a national grid power station is yet to be converted to CHP. The now defunct Battersea Power Station ran on a CHP principle which illustrates that it is feasible. But the cost of converting existing power stations and laying the pipe system is likely to be prohibitive, and small-scale CHP schemes have much more potential. Denmark, which has invested heavily in CHP, has taken the systems to rural villages and outlying suburbs, not just the cities and towns, proof that it is a workable technology.

Minichips are the miniature version of CHP; 508 units have been installed in the UK at 337 sites, potential sites number 4,200. They are extremely economic and can run as a single generator, providing heat, hot water and electricity, or as part of a district heating system where a network of houses or commercial buildings are linked up. They can run off gas, coal, oil, electricity or even waste.

As well as making power stations more efficient, electrical appliances and living and work spaces can be improved too. In the FoE report to the House of Lords, a number of energy-inefficient appliances were isolated and examined. FoE pinpointed fridges, light bulbs, washing machines, dishwashers, televisions, and tumble driers as energy wasters. Instead of more energy being made available for more gadgets, it makes sense to cut the energy needs of these appliances and, in the words of FoE, create 'negawatts' instead of megawatts.

Energy Breakdown of Appliances Used in the UK (1986)

Appliance	Average Gigawatt	%
Refrigerators	0.6	13
Fridge-freezers	0.4	8
Freezers	0.9	18
Colour/mono TV's	0.8	19
Washing machines	0.4	9
Clothes driers	0.1	3
Dishwashers	0.1	2
Vacuum cleaners	0.1	1
Electric blankets	0.1	1
Irons	0.2	4
Electric kettles	0.5	11
Other	0.4	9
TOTAL	4.3	100

Source: Efficiency of Electricity Use, Friends of the Earth

Domestic appliances use just under half of the electricity supplied to homes. Out of that figure, televisions use the most power (19 per cent), followed by freezers (18 per cent), then refrigerators (13 per cent). Vacuum cleaners and electric blankets are the lowest identified users (one per cent each). FoE concluded that 75 per cent electricity savings could be made by introducing more efficient appliances.

Proportions of fuel used in 'average' house

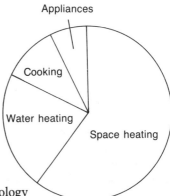

Appliances

Cooking

Water heating

Space heating

Source: Centre for Alternative Technology

The average freezer on sale in the UK today uses 610kWh of electricity per year; mass-produced equivalents sold in Germany use only 180kWh per year, but are not available here. FoE calculated that replacing old, worn-out fridges and freezers with energy efficient models over the next 15 years would wipe out the need for 1.8GW of electricity. (As a comparison, if Hinkley Point C nuclear power station is built it will have a generating capacity of 1.2GW.)

The new generation of fridges and freezers keep food fresher and have much better insulation. For example, the specialist Sun Frost range keeps food fresh for weeks rather than days if a power cut occurs. They also have a life of 30 to 40 years. If this sort of technology was introduced into commercial-sized refrigeration plants, they could be turned off during peak times and then switched back on during low demand periods, saving money for the companies that own them and using less energy.

Lighting our houses, workplaces and public buildings may account for over 10GW of power at peak time — this could be cut by 75 per cent if new fluorescent lamps were used instead of the incandescent light bulb. These new lamps last five times longer and need less than 20 per cent of the power used by an ordinary light bulb. In the Halls of Residence at Edinburgh University, 750 conventional 100 watt light bulbs were replaced with compact fluorescent lamps; after one year the University had saved £17,000. Research into fluorescent tube lighting, used widely in commercial and public buildings, has made it possible to save over 90 per cent of electricity.

The average UK washing machine uses 400kWh per year, but could use as little as 40kWh with no reduction in cleaning ability. By spinning clothes so that they only contained 35 per cent moisture level instead of 80 per cent would save up to two thirds of the energy used in a tumble dryer. And in relation to the greenhouse effect, FoE has calculated that by using energy-efficient fridges, freezers, domestic lighting and washing machines, the annual UK emission of carbon dioxide would be cut by 17.5 million tonnes.

Efficiency matters

Real progress, but only if such appliances are available in Britain — at the moment the majority are not. It is therefore crucial that standards are set by the EEC and that manufacturers, government and retailers should be forced to provide the best technology on the market. In addition, a thorough, comparative labelling system must be set up to reveal the most wasteful appliances.

Badly insulated buildings and houses are another prime area for improvement. Buildings use up around half the energy consumed in the UK; an ordinary semi-detached house uses, on average, 22,000kWh of energy per year. Space heating uses well over half, yet 75 per cent of it escapes into the outside world. The Centre for Alternative Technology (CAT) has worked out that, on average, 20 per cent of heating goes through the roof, 25 per cent through the walls, 10 per cent through the floor, 10 per cent through the windows and 10 per cent in draughts. No wonder your heating bills are so high!

Where 75% of your heating costs go

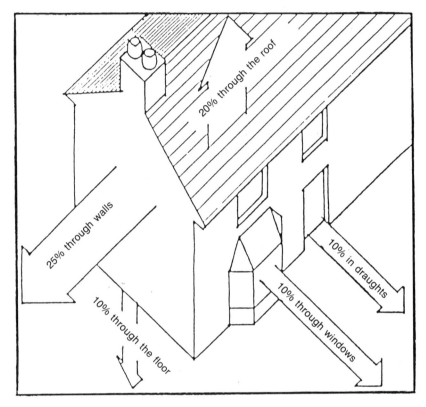

Source: Centre for Alternative Technology

By taking six simple steps you could make your home snug for half the price. CAT has devised a programme in order of priority to save 80 per cent of wasted energy:

1. Reduce thermostat temperature to 18°C or 65°F (each degree increase increases energy consumption by 10 per cent). This saves 17 per cent.
2. Draughtstrip doors and windows, reduce draughts from fireplaces and skirting boards. This saves 11 per cent.
3. Insulate the loft with 100-500mm (4"-6") thick insulating material. This saves 8 per cent.
4. Insulate walls with cavity filler. This saves 16 per cent.
5. Fit heavy, lined curtains on all windows. This saves 3 per cent.
6. Double glaze windows, add lobbies to outside doors. This saves 25 per cent.

Milton Keynes is Britain's foremost energy-efficient town. Its building standards are far higher than present UK Building Regulations, and every new building has to comply. One thousand buildings have been constructed to these standards at costs of one per cent more but with a resulting 40 per cent cut in heating bills. The secret is better insulation, high efficiency gas condensing boilers, individual room heating controls and passive solar heating from large south facing windows. The Scandinavian countries are already streets ahead in this area.

The majority of vehicles pounding the British countryside produce four times their own weight in carbon dioxide every year. The country's 22.5 million cars emit 20 per cent of total carbon dioxide emissions. The average car engine is only 15 per cent efficient. Greater fuel efficiency is essential and there are now prototype cars that can travel between 52 and 100 miles per gallon. Some campaigners believe that the Government should place a limit on the number of cars allowed into cities, such as London, to ease congestion and pollution. Better public transport is essential to save energy.

Nuclear power

Despite the major savings that can be made through relatively simple actions, the government largely ignores the possibilities. Funding to the Energy Efficiency Office has been cut by half. The Office has stopped subsidising one-day energy surveys for industry and commerce and there is little accessible public information. In some states of America, utility companies have to sponsor energy efficiency by law, and a home energy survey is free to every household. The House of Commons Energy Select Committee believes that the Government is not doing enough to promote energy efficiency.

The promotion of energy conservation and energy efficiency could play a much bigger part in cleaning up the environment than any other measure the government can take. What I am concerned about is that electricity privatisation will not lend itself to improving the situation.
David Clelland MP, House of Commons Energy Select Committe.

The Electricity Privatisation Bill states that working up to the year 2000 supply companies must buy between 15 and 20 per cent of their energy from non-fossil fuel resources. This sounds like an invitation to buy from renewable technologies until you realise that the intended non-fossil fuel source is nuclear power. Renewable energy is to provide only one per cent of electricity by the end of the century.

The Government still believes that nuclear power is the energy of the future that will keep the lights shining brightly and at low cost. It has also adopted nuclear power as a solution to the greenhouse effect. Since the 1950s, £16 billion has been spent on nuclear research and development, which is equivalent to a one and a quarter pence tax on each unit of nuclear electricity produced over the years. In comparison only £150 million has been spent on renewables since the 1970s. In the year 1988/89, £256.8 million went to the nuclear industry, and only £16 million on renewables.

Nuclear power stations are notoriously unreliable and construction costs go way over original estimates. In 1965 the first advanced gas cooled reactor, Dungeness B, was ordered. Seventeen years later in 1982 the first reactor started up, and the second one in 1985. By the end of 1988 the lifetime output was calculated to be less than 22 per cent of its original design capacity.

There are proposals for three more nuclear power stations to be built in Britain during the next decade: Hinckley Point C, Wylfa B and Sizewell C. And there may be plans to build a total of ten extra nuclear power stations by 2010. One consideration is that supplies of uranium, the basic fuel of a nuclear reactor will run out, probably within the next 60 to 90 years.

> *The Government needs to follow a much more aggressive programe to promote renewable technologies. If it's left to the free market these things will not progress fast enough.*
> Michael Flood, Energy Consultant.

Apart from inefficiency and vast costs, nuclear power has two additional threats: accidents and radioactive waste. During the last 30 years there have been 12 accidents around the world that have caused serious damage to a reactor core. The most publicised of these were Three Mile Island in America (1979) and Chernobyl in Russia (1986). The effects of the Chernobyl radiation leak were measured all over Europe, 32 people died as a result of fighting the fire that occurred, and thousands more are expected to develop cancers as a result of radioactive contamination. A total of 135,000 Russian people were evacuated from a 100km radius around the accident zone. These accidents resulted from a technology that is supposed to be failsafe.

The amount of high level radioactive waste kept at Sellafield Reprocessing plant is estimated to be 1200 meters cubed and the figure is expected to double by the end of the century. No one has yet solved the problem of what to do with it — turning it into glass chips is the latest idea, but engineers have to wait between 30 and 50 years until the waste has cooled down sufficiently enough for the process to take place.

High level waste remains active for 250,000 years and is highly toxic to most life forms. Even low level waste stays radioactive for 300 years. The Irish Sea is reputed to be the most radioactive in the world. Environmentalists estimate that a quarter of a tonne of plutonium has been deposited in the area from two million gallons of radioactive effluents that have poured out from Sellafield.

There has always been a strongly suspected link between nuclear power stations and leukaemia and malignant lymphomas. Studies by the Independent Committee on Medical Aspects of Radiation in the Environment have already indicated that clusters of cancer (particularly childhood cancers) occur around nuclear power stations and a recent report by Somerset Health Authority confirms that. Levels around Hinkley Point are nearly twice the national average and, between 1969 and 1973, cases of cancer were four times higher than the national average in people under the age of 25 living in a radius of 12.5km around Hinkley Point.

Alternative power
Given these disturbing facts, the phasing out of nuclear power and phasing in of renewable technologies makes sense. The Government's most favourable estimate for renewable power is that it could be providing 10 per cent by 2025. It argues that renewable energies are not developed enough for a higher goal, but if more money for research was made available, the future could be very different. Michael Flood, an independent energy consultant, has concluded in a study done for Friends of the Earth that 20 per cent of our power could come from renewable sources within 50 years. Already UK companies have developed some of the best technology in the world and are exporting to other countries. Are the renewables always to be the Cinderella option?

Why should they be? Britain is packed with energy sources. Not only do we have our own supplies of coal, oil and gas, we also have some of the best wind and wave conditions in the world. Wind power and passive solar are competitive with the cost of nuclear power. So far, the most successful renewable energy plants have been the ten hydro electric stations in Scotland providing around 2 per cent of the country's electricity.

> *The British Government still regards renewable energy as the Cinderella option, particularly when it moves from research to commerical options.*
> Stewart Boyle, Association for the Conservation of Energy.

Denmark, Sweden, Greece, America, China and India are just some of the countries which have widespread renewable technologies running commercially. India has 30 villages supplying all their energy from renewable sources — providing jobs and cheap power. The beauty of renewable energy is that it doesn't rely on one source only, such as wind or solar, but on a whole range of different sources. One wind turbine at Trimblemill on the Isle of Thurso, Scotland, only produces 7kW of power a year, but that is still enough to provide electricity for lights and appliances for the island population.

Wind
There are over 40 wind turbines (50kW upwards) currently in operation in the UK and the Government plans to set up another three wind 'farms' at Langdon Common in Scotland, Capel Cynon in Wales and Cold Northcott in Cornwall. Each farm will have 25 turbines generating between 300-400kW each. There are already hundreds of small battery charging turbines (50kW downwards) in private ownership. In Denmark, private investors have been successfully encouraged to build their own small wind turbines and now wind

accounts for one per cent of electricity consumed there. California, one of the most energy conscious areas in the world, has an installed capacity of over 1500MW, more than the provision offered by a medium sized power station. California's wind turbines provide one per cent of electricity and is equal to 80 per cent of the world's total installed capacity for wind energy.

Wind farms near Palm Springs, California.

Wind sites must be placed where the wind blows fairly constantly, most of them are situated around the coast. At the moment, only inshore wind farms have been erected but there is great potential in offshore wind. Offshore wind farms would be more expensive to establish but far less of an eyesore. Offshore also has the added advantage of non-stop wind.

Wind turbines can generate electricity for the local community or be part of the national grid, such as the Orkney Islands and Carmarthen Bay. Wind speeds of 9mph begin to produce worthwhile power, and turbines should be chosen to suit the average speed of the winds. A wrong choice could ruin the turbine because of high winds or not produce enough energy because of low winds. Wind power can be used to great effect in Third World countries and outlying areas to pump water, to drive diesel engines and to store electricity in batteries.

Solar

The sun beams down an astonishing amount of energy to our planet — one year's global energy use in the space of an hour. Countries in the northern hemisphere are frequently covered in cloud even on a warm day, but sunny countries such as Greece and Israel are in ideal locations to make use of active solar power to heat up water, spaces and to create electricity. The sun may not shine that much on Britain but that doesn't exclude us from using solar power. Buildings can be designed to absorb and retain heat from the sun to save on heating costs. It's also possible to use solar power directly to contribute to space and water heating but the snag is the expense — photovoltaic cells which can store solar power used in conjunction with batteries are still quite costly, but with more research prices could become reasonable and give active solar power definite potential.

Passive solar techniques have been used successfully in a number of British buildings. The Pennyland estate in Milton Keynes has over 100 houses that have been designed to catch as much sun as possible, cutting annual heating bills by 40 per cent and costing just one per cent more to build. The Wiggins Teape head office in Basingstoke has a multi-windowed atrium which allows all the offices to be lit by daylight. St George's School in Wallasey doesn't have any heating bills at all; the double glazed south wall provides 50 per cent of the heat needed, lighting 34 per cent, while the other 16 per cent is provided by the bodies of school children.

Solar trickle roof and heat store. Water is heated by sun in summer and used to provide heat in winter.

Features of a passive solar building are large south-facing windows, small north-facing windows, glass conservatories, excellent insulation and use of brick, concrete or stone. Other more specialised techniques are trombe walls and double envelope construction. In trombe walls a sheet of glass is fixed just in front of a blackened, south-facing wall, and the wall absorbs heat through the day which reaches the inner wall by night. In double envelope construction, the living space is contained by an insulated, all-weather shell, between which warm air circulates.

Waste

Waste and what to do with it is an ever growing problem. Each year Britain's domestic, industrial and agricultural wastes amount to some 250 million tonnes. Solid wastes are either burnt or buried in landfill tips and fluid wastes are dumped in the sea. As a whole these wastes are estimated to have an energy equivalent of 21 million tonnes of coal, and government, industry and local authorities alike are very keen on obtaining energy from such cheap sources which are termed biofuels — fuels that come from an organic origin.

Biofuels include crops and trees, sewage and animal slurry, and industrial and domestic wastes. A seventh of the world's energy is already provided by biofuels in the form of firewood and animal dung, particularly in Third World countries who cannot afford to rely on fossil fuels.

Domestic refuse can be burned to produce heat and electricity — we produce 25 million tonnes per year. Currently 95 per cent of it is buried in landfill sites at an annual average of half a tonne of rubbish per household. There are up to 360 incinerators working abroad and Britain also has a few systems. For example, an incinerator in Edmonton, North London, burns around 400,000 tons of rubbish every year and provides electricity too. At the Blue Circle Cement Works in Wiltshire, 20 per cent of energy is provided by burning shredded rubbish and rubbish pellets (a more processed version which contains 60 per cent of the calorific value of coal). In Nottingham an incinerator provides heat for 16,000 homes and local industry. A boiler owned by Sun Valley Poultry burns chicken litter. Other schemes exist in Jersey, Sheffield and Newcastle.

Straw burning for energy also has great potential. Each year straw equivalent to 3.6 million tonnes of coal is wasted, usually burnt in the field or ploughed back into the ground. The Department of Energy estimates that by the year 2000, 1.6 million tonnes of straw could be providing energy on farms and for industry. Woburn Abbey has a straw-fired boiler which pumps hot water around the estate with savings of over £20,000 every year.

Offcuts from the wood industry could also be used as fuel. Furniture makers already use an estimated 35,000 tonnes of waste wood to fire boilers for space and water heating. The Department of Energy is looking into the possibilities of growing trees specifically for fuel purposes on land that is no good for agricultural crops.

Producing methane gas from landfill sites, sewage works and organic wastes is another extremely practical use of resources. There are currently around 20 commercial operations in the UK that extract the methane from landfill sites produced by rotting rubbish. Because there is no oxygen in the tips, methane forms, and each tonne of rubbish can produce up to 250 cubic metres of gas over a ten year period. Anaerobic digesters work on a similar principle and are used for creating gas from sewage and other wastes. Some UK sewage farms have run off sludge gas for years, and in China over one million digesters produce methane from human and animal sewage to provide gas for cooking.

Heat from rocks

Geothermal power (heat from rocks) is a technology that is still undergoing research in this country and which is seen by the Government as an energy longshot. The earth's crust contains stratas of hot, dry rock and natural aquifers — pockets or streams of hot water. To extract heat from the rock, two j-shaped boreholes have to be drilled into the rock, several kilometers deep. Then the rock between the boreholes is fractured by high pressure water jets and the heat released, gathered by a circulating stream of water. Aquifers are located and drilled into, so releasing the water trapped in the pockets.

The potential for Britain lies in hot, dry rock rather than aquifers, and areas suitable for energy production would be south-west England, the Lake District, north east England and the Scottish Highlands. The Department of Energy estimates that 10 per cent of our electricity could come from hot dry rock in 125 years' time. For many years Iceland and New Zealand have used geysers and acquifers to provide space and water heating and in Britain research work that began in 1973 on hot dry rock is still continuing at the Camborne School of Mines, Cornwall. We have yet to produce a commercial installation. The energy potential of geothermal power is enormous but research is vital to provide more economical methods of production.

Water

The final renewable technology is water — hydro power taken from dams, tides and waves. Hydro power provides 5.7 per cent of the world's energy and around two per cent of Britain's energy. There are six tidal barrages in existence today and the UK is currently considering a tidal barrage built across the Severn estuary. The Severn estuary's tidal range is 11 metres, the second biggest in the world, and the Department of Energy forecasts that the barrage could provide 8GW of electricity per year. The most serious problem with it is the possible environmental threat to wild-life, particularly fish and wading birds. Other potential sites are the River Mersey, the Solway Firth in Scotland, Morecombe Bay, Padstow, the Humber, Conwy and the Wash. The most likely of these barrages to be built is across the Mersey, which would meet half of Liverpool's electricity needs.

In the eyes of the Department of Energy, wave power on a large scale is uneconomical and it ceased to fund such projects following reviews in 1983 and 1985. Now any research given funding is small scale with the intention of competing with high cost fossil fuels such as diesel. Japan and Norway are both continuing research into wave power, and renewable energy campaigners believe that wave power could still be a major UK power contribution if research was encouraged and subsidised by the Government. Estimates are that waves could supply up to one fifth of our electricity demand.

Overview of renewable energy sources in the area of the North Western Electricity Board (Norweb) 1989

Renewable		Technical	Resource	Economic
Biofuels	Forestry	□	□	□
	Landfill Gas	□	□	□
	General Ind Waste	□	□	□
	Special Ind Waste	□	□	□
	Municipal Waste	□	□	□
Geothermal	Hot Dry Rocks	○	□	○
	Aquifers	□	○	○
Water	Small Scale Hydro	□	□	□
	Tidal	□	□	□
	Wave Inshore	○	○	○
	Wave Offshore	○	□*	○
Wind	Onshore +	□	□	□

Key: □ positive potential
     ○ negative outlook
* Resource not quantified in study
+ Offshore wind energy not considered in study

(*Source:* Norweb and the Energy Technology Support Unit for the Department of Energy.)

It is encouraging to see that some organisations are taking renewable energy seriously. The North Western Electricity Board (Norweb) recently published a report on renewable sources in its area, and is the first electricity board to do so. Norweb stated that the small scale sizes of renewable energy sources made them highly suitable for local integration and concluded that 12 per cent of electricity demand could be generated from these sources. The Board also said that there was a substantially greater potential, but at a higher cost. The only technologies considered to be difficult to implement were wave power, hot dry rocks and aquifers, although they have adequate supplies of hot dry rocks. Biofuels and wind power are regarded as the most promising technologies, along with small scale hydro and tidal power.

The future for energy production in Britain could be very bright indeed. The UK has the potential to be at the forefront of efficiency and renewables. Our islands offer excellent all-round resources, particularly wind, wave, tidal and waste. But the as yet unanswered question remains — does the political and commercial will to change our ways exist? The Government is at the crossroads. Do we go nuclear? Do we carry on burning fossil fuels at rapid rates? Do we embrace energy efficiency? Do we aggressively develop renewable resources? The last two options working in harmony make perfect sense. The decisions taken now will affect numerous generations, not just our own, and as well as the Government it is up to us, the consumers, to adopt our own energy policies before it's too late.

Take Action

In the home
— insulate your house properly
— use room by room thermostats for central heating
— make sure you have a highly efficient gas condensing boiler
— use long life fluorescent bulbs in your light fittings
— switch off lights when you are not using them

In the shops
— Don't forget to ask how much energy an appliance uses in a year and do your own comparison with similar appliances
— buy a car with a high mileage per gallon

The Government
— introduce an accurate energy labelling system on appliances
— encourage retailers and manufacturers to supply the best technology at mass market prices and availability
— stipulate that electricity utility companies have to sponsor energy efficiency
— continue publicising energy efficiency to domestic consumers and industry
— cut back spending on nuclear research programmes, in order to concentrate on renewable sources of energy and their commercial introduction.

Chapter 3

Acid Rain

In April 1974 the rainfall in Pitlochry, Scotland, had an acidity level close to lemon juice. In late 1978 the town of Wheeling, West Virginia, experienced a shower equivalent to stomach fluid. In February 1984 the strange, black snow that fell on the Scottish Cairngorms bore more resemblance to vinegar than frozen water.

The phenomenon was acid rain, the culprits were interacting airborne chemical compounds. Waste emissions of sulphur dioxide (SO_2) and nitrogen oxides (NOx) from power stations, industry and car exhausts. The victim was the natural environment — water, soil and a multitude of dependent ecosystems.

Acid rain was first officially recorded in 1872 by Robert Smith, Britain's first pollution officer. In his book *Air and Rain*, Smith observed that there was a link between the blackened skies of industrial Manchester and acidic rainfall. Despite Smith's enlightening discovery no one followed up the connection until the 1960s when Swedish scientists recorded a high rate of fish deaths in the southern lakes of their country. They concluded that the indigenous perch, pike, trout, salmon and Arctic char populations were dying because of increasingly acidic water.

What the scientists had come across were the grim results of continuous and uncontrolled air pollution, present in varying levels from the beginning of the Industrial Revolution. Sulphur emissions from coal-fired power stations shot up after World War II due to growing energy demands, and reached a peak in the 1970s. Today, emissions are overall lower but remain too high for sensitive ecosystems to bear.

> *We should not gamble with the quality of our air. It is our life support system and the life support system of the whole globe. Because of that, it is important that we take the right steps at the right time to ensure the right results.*
> Nicholas Ridley, former Secretary of State for the Environment.

Acid rain forms when airborne sulphur dioxide and nitrogen oxides go through a series of complex atmospheric reactions and are turned into weak sulphuric and nitric acids contained in rain drops. Carried by strong winds the rain is capable of travelling hundreds, even thousands of miles, from as far away as the USA to Britain. Consequently countries can 'export' and 'import' acid rain, regardless of national barriers. If the SO_2 and NOx do not react with water droplets, they fall back to earth in the form of a dry deposition of gas or particles. Dry deposition rarely falls beyond a 300km radius from its original source and has more effect on the immediate locality.

Effects of acid rain

When acid rain falls it affects the pH balance of the soil and the water in rivers and lakes. Like human skin, they have a natural balance between acidity and alkalinity which is measured on the pH scale (from 0, near battery acid, to 14, equivalent to caustic soda). A pH balance of seven is neutral. Normally rain is slightly acidic at pH 5.6, but emissions of sulphur and nitrogen oxides cause it to lower to a pH of 5 or less. A freshwater lake in normal conditions should have a pH of between 6 and 7 but acidified lakes can have a pH reading of as low as 3.5.

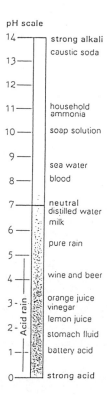

pH scale

pH	
14	strong alkali
	caustic soda
13	
12	
11	household ammonia
10	soap solution
9	
	sea water
8	blood
7	neutral
	distilled water
	milk
6	
	pure rain
5	
4	wine and beer
	orange juice
3	vinegar
	lemon juice
2	stomach fluid
1	battery acid
0	strong acid

(Acid rain range: pH 0 to 5)

Source: World Wide Fund for Nature

The pH balance of soil varies from place to place and among other factors depends on the bedrock beneath. Nutrients vital to tree health, such as calcium, magnesium, sodium and potassium, are easily leached out when a high level of acidity occurs. Too much acidity also makes aluminium more soluble (the most common metal to be found in the earth's crust). Once aluminium passes into the water system it is toxic to fish, and may find its way into human drinking systems.

Soils based on limestone or sandstone are naturally more alkaline, and because of their high calcium content are better equipped to buffer the effects of dry and wet acid deposition. Scandinavia, which has the biggest concentration of acidified lakes in Europe, has thin top soil based on granite bedrock, as has Scotland, north west Cumbria, the Pennines and Wales where freshwater acidification is also prevalent.

As a lake becomes more acidified, so more of its inhabitants begin to die out. The first creatures to disappear are crayfish, snails and mussels, certain types of plankton, mayflies, caddis flies, followed by salmon, trout and pike. Without fish, insects become the dominant species and acid-loving insects, such as water boatmen, proliferate. Loss of fish, of course, has an effect on fish-eating birds and in Scandinavia and North America ospreys and divers are declining due to lack of food.

Freshwater life is also at risk from what is known as 'acid pulse'. This occurs in cold climates that have heavy snowfalls during the winter. When the snow melts in the springtime, huge quantities of concentrated acidified water flush into the streams and rivers and can cause large scale fish kills, even in areas of buffered soil.

Other airborne pollutants that combine with acid rain are tropospheric ozone (see Chapter 4) and ammonia. Tropospheric ozone (not to be confused with the ozone layer) forms when vehicle emissions react with sunlight and is widely believed to damage trees. Although it is not acidic, ozone damages the cellular makeup of plants and trees and, together with sulphur dioxide and nitrogen oxides, forms clouds of polluted air. In California, pines suffer from yellowish flecking due to ozone pollution and Los Angeles is notorious for its thick ozone smogs.

Ammonia (a compound of nitrogen) contributes to both acidification and nitrogen saturation in the soil. It is often a by-product of intensive livestock rearing and is created by large quantities of animal slurry which is disposed of inadequately. The Netherlands, which has an enormous pig farming industry, suffers badly from ammonia pollution.

Examples of damage from all these pollutants are numerous. In Canada, thousands of maple trees are showing damage from air pollution. This could be the result of sulphur emissions from the largest nickel and copper smelting plant in the world which is based in Sudbury, Ontario. Each year it belches out the sum of 325,000 tonnes of sulphur. The phenomenon of crumbling historic buildings, greatly accelerated in the twentieth century, is also attributed to the blight of acid rain. The Parthenon in Athens, St Paul's

Cathedral in London and the Leaning Tower of Pisa are just a few priceless examples.

Because the individual effects of acidification, ozone pollution, climate and insect and fungal attacks are so difficult to isolate, there is some disagreement among experts as to the cause of ill health in trees. However, most researchers agree that the multiple stress of all these factors cause tree damage and, in a small percentage of cases, tree death.

Dead tree in foreground with cooling towers of Trent Valley Power Station beyond.

The symptoms of tree damage are 'crown die-back' when the top of the tree is not as bushy as it should be, and include broken branches, undeveloped buds and shoots, deformed branches, defoliation and discoloured leaves and needles. Damage tends to be measured in needle or leaf defoliation — a tree can suffer up to 60 per cent defoliation and still recover.

In the Erz Gebirge mountain range spanning the Czech/East German border, a substantial acreage has been decimated by acidification, both from direct exposure to sulphur dioxide and from acid rain. Some of the top soil is so acidic that no tree can survive and the Government has resorted to digging up the affected soil and replacing it with fresh stocks. The Black Forest in Germany has been the victim of forest decline, where symptoms such as yellowing leaves and needles and a thinning crown affect half the country's trees.

Who emits what?

In 1987, Europe emitted an estimated 21.4 million tonnes of sulphur and 19.5 million tonnes of nitrogen dioxide. Of those figures, Britain contributed 1.84 million tonnes of sulphur and an equal amount of nitrogen dioxide. The worldwide yearly sulphur output is estimated to be between 50 and 75 million tonnes and is concentrated in the industrial regions. This amount is equalled by naturally forming sulphur that originates mainly from volcanoes and huge clusters of marine bacteria.

On their own, natural emissions of sulphur are fairly harmless and can nourish crops and create a barrier to fungal infestations. But a combination of natural and man-made sulphur results in overload for sensitive ecosystems. In Europe 90 per cent of sulphur deposition is man-made, making levels ten times greater than they should be.

Grangemouth Petrochemical Complex beyond farmland at Kinneil Kerse. Atmospheric pollution is clearly visible.

Nitrogen oxide emissions from vehicles are rising every year because of the huge growth in the number of cars. In 1950 there were 50 million cars and vans in the world, now there are 400 million. Exhaust fumes can be made cleaner by the installation of three-way catalytic converters which significantly reduce waste emissions (see Chapter 5).

Fifteen major SO$_2$ polluters in Europe with more than 200,000 tons SO$_2$ emissions per year.

Emitter	Country	Capacity (MW)	Emissions (tons SO$_2$)
1. Puentes	Spain	1400	632.000
2. Boxberg	German Democratic Republic	3250	459.000
3. Andorra	Spain	1050	407.000
4. Balti/Eesti	USSR (Estonian SSR)	3100	386.000
5. Drax	United Kingdom	3960	337.000
6. Petsamo	USSR (Kola peninsula)		337.000
7. Schwarze Pumpe	German Democratic Republic	1050	320.000
8. Prunerov	Czechoslovakia	1710	280.000
9. Hagenwerder	German Democratic Republic	1700	263.000
10. Melnik	Czechoslovakia	1270	260.000
11. Balchatow	Poland		254.000
12. Tusinice	Czechoslovakia	1460	230.000
13. Turow	Poland		227.000
14. Janschwalde	German Democratic Republic	2500	208.000
15. Severo	USSR (Kola peninsula)		200.000

Source: Stop Acid Rain Campaign.

Britain tops the league for sulphur emissions in Western Europe, but the Eastern block — Russia, East Germany, Poland and Czechoslovakia are by far the worst offenders. They obtain 70 per cent of their energy from burning coal, usually the brown variety, which has a high sulphur content and a low energy value. The East German power station of Janschwalde burns 30 million tonnes of coal per year and annually emits as much sulphur dioxide as Sweden. At present the EEC is considering donating financial or technological aid to Poland, East Germany and Czechoslovakia to help reduce emissions. West Germany has already begun its aid programme.

Since the 1970s Scandinavia, and in particular Sweden and Norway, has been campaigning for other countries to drastically cut sulphur and nitrogen oxide emissions. The two countries' joint campaigning body, Stop Acid Rain, is unremitting in its promotion of the case against acid rain. For over three decades these two countries have been the unwilling recipients of acid rain 'export' on a massive scale. Ninety per cent of their acid deposition is caused by other countries. Based on 1987 European Monitoring and Evaluation (EMEP) figures, the UK was responsible for 10 per cent of the sulphur deposition that fell on Norway.

> *If reductions aren't made big enough and quick enough, acidification will continue further north in Scandinavia and no one knows how long it will take the ground to recover.*
> Christer Agren, Swedish Environmental Protection Board.

Two-thirds of Sweden is vulnerable to acid rain because of its bedrock and geographical position, lying beneath the prevailing winds. The effects have been devastating — out of 100,000 lakes in Sweden, 16,000 are acidified and 4,000 are fishless. In Southern Norway, lakes in a region of 18,000sq km are virtually devoid of fish, while salmon have vanished from seven major rivers. An acidified lake looks very still and clear but is an animal and plant graveyard.

Legislation

In 1976 Norway held the first international conference on the effects of acidification, and a year later put forward the proposal to set up a convention to control emissions of sulphur dioxide and thereby reduce transboundary pollution. In 1979 the ensuing Convention on Long-range Transboundary Air Pollution (CLRTAP), drawn up by the United Nations Economic Commission for Europe (UN ECE), was signed by 34 countries including all Western and Eastern European states, America and Canada. It came into force in March 1983 after two thirds of the signing countries had ratified it.

The initial agreement was a statement of principle rather than a binding promise, whereby it was agreed that countries should make every effort to 'use the best available technology that is economically feasible' to limit air pollution. One of the first steps taken was to set up the European Monitoring and Evaluation Programme (EMEP) to measure emissions and deposition of sulphur and nitrogen oxides in Europe. The aim was to create a non-biased set of figures that would paint an international picture of the scale of air pollution.

In 1983, in an effort to get the ball rolling on realistic cuts, the Scandinavian countries proposed a 30 per cent reduction in sulphur emissions by 1993, using 1980 as the baseline year. West Germany, Switzerland, Austria and Canada all welcomed the proposal and, along with Scandinavia, became known as the Thirty Per Cent Club. The hard campaigning continued and two years later, in 1985, 21 countries signed the Helsinki Protocol, a legally binding agreement equivalent to the demands of the Thirty Per Cent Club. The UK and America refused to sign, claiming that more research was needed before allowing any definite reduction. Instead, Mrs Thatcher pledged to reduce total SO_2 emissions by 30 per cent by the year 2000.

Who belongs to the thirty per cent club? And what have they promised?

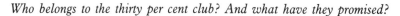

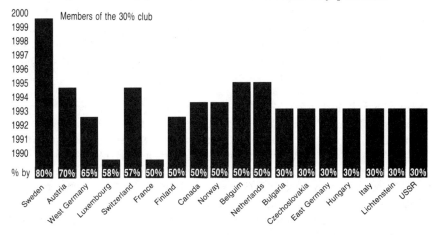

Source: Stop Acid Rain Campaign

The EEC has taken a direct interest in the problem of acid deposition, and in November 1988 a directive was agreed upon by EEC environment ministers concerning the sulphur emissions of large combustion plants. It was aimed at power stations, metal manufacturers, waste disposal units, chemical works and the food industry — some of the biggest emitters of sulphur. Using 1980 as the base year, sulphur dioxide reduction aims are as follows: 20 per cent by 1993, 40 per cent by 1998 and 60 per cent by 2003.

Limiting emissions of nitrogen oxides is also an important step, and in 1988 a further United Nations Protocol to control NOx was signed by 25 countries (including the UK) in Bulgaria. Signatories must freeze NOx emissions by

1995 (using 1987 as the baseline year). Undoubtedly, EEC legislation to fit all new cars with catalytic converters by 1990 will help.

Some countries are keener on being cleaner than others and it has been left up to the badly affected states of Europe to set the best example. Sweden, Austria and West Germany plan to cut total SO_2 emissions by between 65 and 70 per cent by the year 1995 and Sweden hopes to reach an 80 per cent reduction by the end of the century.

Each year, Sweden spends £10 million on liming acidified lakes to neutralise acidity, but the programme is limited to 4,000 lakes and rivers. Liming programmes have been carried out in Scotland, Cumbria and Wales. However this is a very expensive technique and a fast flowing stream or river may have to be limed continuously, and a lake every three to five years. Sweden is conducting experimental research on liming forest areas too. In the UK the majority of lime deposits lie in the National Parks, which brings its own environmental problems.

In 1982 West Germany discovered it had serious problems with its forests — results of research indicated that half showed signs of ill health. By 1984, half the supply of spruce, pine, beech and oak had some degree of unnatural damage. Acidification was no longer a Scandinavian aberration. Over the last five years 50 per cent of Germany's energy producing capacity has been equipped with flue gas desulphurisation systems (FGD) which removes the bulk of sulphur before it even reaches the chimney. As a nation, the Germans have spent billions cleaning up their act.

The British legacy

Despite promises of reductions in sulphur, the British Government has yet to make much progress. Only one third of one power station is expected to be on-line with an FGD system by 1994, with a total phase-in by 1996. Current proposals are to retrofit 6,000 MW of power by 1997. The government is intending to convert Drax power station in Yorkshire, and perhaps Ferrybridge in the same county, with FGD.

But there is grave doubt among environmentalists as to whether the Government will fulfil its promises according to schedule. Any new coal-fired power stations built will also be fitted with FGD or a similar technology. Retrofitting with FGD is very expensive but the fact remains that, by the year 2000, the UK will still have 39 coal-fired power stations without clean-up technologies.

There is growing evidence to suggest, however, that acid deposition and ozone pollution are taking their toll on the UK environment. In 1986, out of a total of 655,000 tonnes of sulphur deposited on Britain, 517,000 tonnes originated from indigenous power stations and industry. A total of 80 per cent of our sulphur deposition was home grown.

Independent studies by the Acid Waters Review Group, sponsored by the Department of the Environment, the University of London and Greenpeace, all point to the same conclusion — that Britain does have acidified lakes.

Leading scientists from the Acid Waters Review Group recommended that a 90 per cent cut in acidic deposition is necessary to bring the affected freshwater lakes and streams back to normal. Many lakes have suffered a pH drop of between 1 and 1.5, making them at least ten times more acidic than they should be.

In 1988 Greenpeace published *Acid Waters*, a report by consultant scientist Andrew Tickle. The report surveyed current and past research on the effects of acidification on lakes and rivers. Tickle had four categories into which he classified these waters: acidified, vulnerable, fishless and fish decline. He found that six lakes were fishless, including five lochs in the Galloway area, 24 lakes were acidified in Scotland, Cumbria, Wales and Southern England, 37 lakes were vulnerable in all the above areas, and ten waters showed fish loss, in particular the River Esk in Cumbria and the River Forth in Scotland. Through the report, Tickle illustrated how widespread the problem is.

Figures from the forest report of the UN ECE 1989 show that over 64 per cent of all tree species in the UK have slight to severe defoliation. Britain has the second highest percentage of tree damage after Czechoslovakia. The UK Forestry Commission would take issue with the findings of the UN ECE because they are doubtful of the methods used to measure damage. But the Commission's own surveys show that our trees are not as healthy as they should be, although they are unwilling to lay the blame wholly on acid deposition and ozone pollution without further scientific proof. The Commission holds the view that tree damage is caused by multiple stresses and that air pollution is just one factor.

> *The general consensus of opinion is that there are a number of stresses that affect trees, including climate, frost, drought, insects, fungi and unnatural air pollution. We can't control the climate but we can control the air pollution.*
> Andrew Tickle, Greenpeace.

Concern has been voiced over the plight of the Dipper, a bird which lives near upland rivers in the north and the west of the country. Its current scarcity and decreased egg laying in Wales and Galloway is thought to be the result of lack of appropriate food. The Dipper's main prey are caddis fly larvae and mayfly nymphs which are fast disappearing because they cannot live in acid waters. Otters are also a rare sight near such areas, probably due to lack of fish. Research has shown that frogs and toads are at risk from acidified habitats. High aluminium levels can produce abnormal tadpoles and may suppress growth.

There is no point in sticking our heads in the sand — acid rain and its related pollutants are directly affecting the health of our environment. Whatever the theories, scientists and campaigners agree on one thing; that, if the means of reducing air pollution are available then it should be done. Substantial reductions are possible, as the technology already exists. What is needed is enforcement and funding. To avoid further damage to sensitive ecosystems, sulphur and nitrogen oxide emissions must be cut by 90 per cent. With swift action and investment from all the industrialised nations, acid rain could become a thing of the past.

Take Action

You

— think twice before using your car and have it fitted with a catalytic converter
— conserve energy in the home

The Government

— join the Thirty Per Cent Club and promise to reduce sulphur emissions by 30 per cent by 1993
— offer tax incentives for all older models of cars to be fitted with a catalytic converter
— introduce flue gas desulphurisation or similar systems to more power stations.

Chapter 4

The Ozone Layer

In 1987, the British public became aware of a new dimension in the natural world — the ozone layer. High up in the sky was a protective layer of gas that screened out dangerous ultraviolet rays from the sun. And it had a hole in it. The revelation made front page news. Prince Charles set an example to the nation and banned all aerosols from Highgrove and 'ozone friendly' became an everyday phrase. The discovery of the 'hole' signalled the start of the green consumer revolution.

The Earth's atmosphere

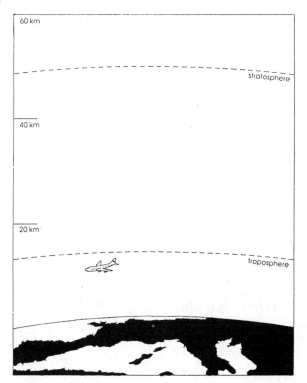

Source: UNEP

The 'hole' was not in fact a new phenomenon. Since the 1970s, scientists had observed a significant depletion in ozone levels over the Antarctic. But in 1987 the British Antarctic Survey witnessed the worst depletion ever recorded during the Antarctic springtime (August, September and October). On some occasions over the three months the concentration of ozone fell by 95 per cent. The observation shocked the world into action and convinced scientists and governments alike that ozone depletion was a serious problem.

> *The atmosphere is the common property of every nation on earth. And unless all nations commit themselves to the elimination of ozone-depleting chemicals, the agreement is compromised. And the environment does not tolerate compromise.*
> Mostafa Tolbe, Executive Director of UNEP.

Further investigations by teams of scientists from all over the world have since laid the blame on man-made chlorinated substances that remain in the atmosphere for 100 years or more, where they destroy ozone. Chlorofluorocarbons (commonly known as CFCs) are the biggest culprits; their main uses are in aerosols as propellants, in foam plastics as an expansion agent, in refrigerators and air conditioning systems as coolants and in-sulators, and as cleaners and degreasers in the electronics industry.

CFCs were developed in the 1930s and were hailed as a triumph of science — they were cheap, non-flammable, non-toxic and reacted with very few other substances. Since that time, a range of CFCs has been developed and identified with numbers, hence you will read about CFC 11, 12, 13, 113, 114 and 115. The numbers simply serve to indicate that each type of CFC has an individual molecular structure.

Halons, which are used in fire extinguishers to quell fire, have a similar effect if left to scavenge in the atmosphere. And so, too, do carbon tetra-chloride and methyl chloroform. Carbon tetrachloride is used in dry cleaning and industrial cleaning, but mainly as an intermediate ingredient in the process for manufacturing CFCs. Methyl chloroform (recognised on pro-ducts as 1' 1' 1' Trichloroethane) is widely used in industry as a solvent and in DIY products and materials for lay-out artists.

All these substances have the ability to float from the lower atmosphere (the troposphere) into the upper atmosphere (the stratosphere) where ozone depletion takes place. Ozone is dispersed throughout the atmosphere but has its highest concentrations between 20 and 30 kilometers above the Earth's surface in the stratosphere, and even then only one molecule out of every 100,000 is ozone.

Essential functions

Survival on a world without ozone would be impossible. The ozone layer screens out the sun's harmful rays and serious depletion could severely affect human health, causing more skin cancer, eye cataracts and premature aging. In addition, it may cause crop damage and disturbances to the marine food chain. Figures from the US Environmental Protection Agency are staggering. They predict that if no controls are placed on CFC and halon emissions there will be over 150 million extra cases of skin cancer in white US citizens born before 2075.

The ozone layer (spread out between 12 and 50km above the Earth), has always existed and, left to its own devices, will regenerate and interact with other airborne gases to create a perfect balance. Unfortunately, ground level ozone (tropospheric) caused by pollution cannot rise up and plug the hole, but instead is harmful and can cause breathing difficulties.

The Antarctic ozone 'hole' in the stratosphere that splashed across the headlines in 1988, has continued to grow and is now the size of the USA. Rather strangely, it only happens during the Antarctic spring. Scientists predict that the hole will continue to appear until chlorine levels fall to those of the mid-70s.

Arctic research

A NASA research team which has recently returned from the Arctic observed a similar pattern of events and is extremely concerned that a second 'hole' may appear over the Arctic. It found that chlorine levels were 50 times higher than they had expected. An ozone depletion over the Arctic could be much more serious, as many more people live closer to the north pole than they do to the south pole; for example North America, Russia and Europe.

The Ozone Trends Panel, a working party of scientists set up in 1986 by NASA, has calculated a three per cent depletion in stratospheric ozone on a global level since 1969. They found that, between the global latitudes of 53 and 64 degrees north, ozone was reduced by up to eight per cent. Included in that zone is anywhere in Britain north of Nottingham and other parts of northern Europe, Russia and Canada.

The undeniable fact is that chlorine is building up in the atmosphere much faster than it can be coped with. Even if chlorine emissions are cut by 50 per cent, scientists have calculated that, by 2050, levels will double. What they cannot be sure of is how the atmosphere will react, and if it will reach a point of no return.

As ozone depletion continues, and the 'holes' become bigger, it is probable that the two poles will be the worst affected regions because of their extreme, but favourable, weather conditions. The increasing depth of the Antarctic ozone hole is closely linked to the phenomenon of the 'polar vortex', a core of very cold air enveloped by strong westerly winds. During the Antarctic winter (our spring) there is little light, and ice clouds form within the vortex. These clouds provide excellent surfaces for chemical reactions to occur upon.

By the time the spring arrives, the region is ideally pre-conditioned for chlorine to break loose from CFCs, halons, methyl chloroform and carbon tetrachloride that has accumulated in the atmosphere. It is estimated that every chlorine molecule has the ability to destroy 100,000 ozone molecules.

Because the chemical reaction between ozone and chlorine lowers the temperature, this makes it even easier for ice clouds to form again the follow-ing winter and the process goes round in a circle. It's also important to realise that air depleted of ozone can travel to other areas through wind currents and transfer the problem.

Since the 1960s there have been big increases in the amounts of CFCs produced and consumed. The global demand is now estimated to be over 1000 million tonnes. The biggest manufacturers of CFCs are the USA, the EEC and Japan. The UK produces ten per cent of world production and consumes five per cent. America has the highest consumption per head in the world and 29 per cent of production, whereas China and India use only two per cent.

It is generally agreed that a reduction of at least 85 per cent in chlorine producing compounds is necessary to keep present atmospheric chlorine levels stable. Only if there was a total ban on CFCs, halons, methyl chloro-form and carbon tetrachloride would ozone depletion decrease. Scientists estimate that the ozone layer would take at least a century to fully recover and regenerate itself. This makes sense when you consider the stored bank of CFCs in products that have not yet been released in the atmosphere. ICI estimates that two years of global production has yet to enter the atmosphere.

Montreal Protocol

Moves to improve the situation began in the 1970s, when in 1976 the UK company, Johnson Wax, banned the use of CFCs in its aerosol products. In 1978 the USA banned the non-essential use of CFCs 11 and 12 in aerosols. In 1982 the EEC limited production of CFCs 11 and 12 and cut their use in aerosols by 30 per cent. But the most cohesive programme to yet be devised has come from the United Nations Environmental Programme (UNEP).

Emissions scenarios for CFCs 11 and 12 until 2050

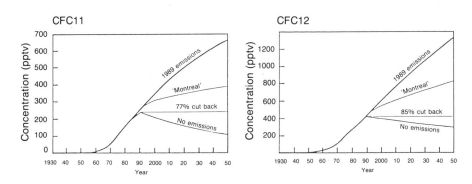

* pptv = parts per trillion volume

Source: Stratospheric Ozone Review Group

In 1977 UNEP set up a co-ordinating committee to review research and calculate projections for ozone depletion. This resulted in the Vienna Convention for the Protection of the Ozone Layer in 1985. Two years later, the Montreal Protocol was launched to cut back CFC and halon emissions. The Protocol has been signed by over 40 countries and came into force at the beginning of 1989. The Protocol demands a freeze on CFCs 11, 12, 113, 114 and 115 at 1986 consumption levels, and a 50 per cent cut by 1999. Consumption of halons 1211, 1301, and 2402 must be frozen by 1992.

But there are loopholes within the Montreal Protocol which must be tightened up to ensure maximum benefit. For a start the Protocol does not cover all the chemicals that deplete the ozone layer. It does not include a ruling on methyl chloroform which accounts for five per cent of depletion and carbon tetrachloride which is responsible for eight per cent.

> *Countless numbers of people are looking to their leaders and representatives to take bold decisions now — and not to put off these critical decisions that will ultimately cause our grandchildren to curse us.*
> The Prince of Wales.

The Protocol also leaves out 'soft' CFCs, which have a much lower potential for ozone depletion but still have a destructive effect. For example, the use of the soft CFC called HCFC 22 is rising rapidly in refrigeration and air conditioning, to replace CFC 12, but it still contains one twentieth of the power of CFC 12 to deplete ozone. And some of these new alternatives also contribute to global warming (see Chapter 1).

Halon production is only required to freeze at 1986 levels by 1992; no direct cuts are to be implemented. But halons have much higher ozone depletion potentials than CFCs 11 and 12, and halon 1301 can live up to 110 years in the atmosphere. They may not be used extensively now, but countries could easily turn to halons as a replacement for some CFCs. The US Environmental Protection Agency has calculated that these unregulated substances could, if they are not incorporated into the Montreal Protocol, account for 40 per cent of stratospheric chlorine levels by 2075.

The Protocol also grant concessions to 'developing countries', allowing the use of 0.3kg of CFCs per person, per year, for a maximum of ten years, but does not make it clear which developing countries are eligible. Friends of the Earth have calculated that if China, India, Indonesia and Brazil took up this concession fully until 1995, global production would have doubled from the 1986 level. Naturally, it is unfair that developing countries should have to forgo the luxuries that make life more comfortable such as fridges and air conditioning, but it is essential that the West makes available the best technology so that they can produce ozone friendly equipment.

Manufacturing countries which did not sign the Protocol include China, India, South Korea, Taiwan and South Africa. It is possible that these countries could become virtual havens for the continuing production of

CFCs. The trade ban between Montreal Protocol countries and other nations in products containing CFCs does not come into force until 1999, which leaves quite a lot of room for quick expansion and sales.

These problems were discussed at the first meeting of the Montreal Protocol Parties in Helsinki in May 1989. It was agreed to tighten the Protocol so that CFC production and consumption would be phased out by the year 2000, and that halon and 'other ozone depleting substances' should be phased out as soon as feasible. The UK also announced a new aid package to India of £40 million pounds for forestry projects and the adoption of non-CFC programmes.

Elimination of CFCs

Environmentalists do not believe that this phase-out is fast enough. For example, the Swedes and the Norwegians are seeking to eliminate CFC use by 1995, and it is possible that the rest of the world could follow suit. Manufacturing companies such as ICI and Du Pont say that it will take between five and seven years to develop suitable alternatives, and in some cases much less, so compliance with a 1995 withdrawal should pose few problems.

The UK British Aerosol Manufacturer's Association has committed its member companies to a 90 per cent reduction in the use of CFCs by 1990, together with a voluntary 'ozone friendly' labelling system. The remaining 10 per cent of CFCs will only be used for 'essential' products, including medical and industrial products. However, environmentalists are calling for proof from manufacturers that no other propellant can be used to replace CFCs in these instances, so that emissions are kept to a bare minimum.

Aerosols which are 'ozone friendly',
ie. lack CFC propellants.

Due to the fact that aerosols have accounted for 60 per cent of CFC usage in the UK, Britain will meet the terms of the Montreal Protocol (a 50 per cent cut in CFCs) ten years ahead of schedule. But that does not mean Britain can rest on its laurels — there is still a long way to go. CFCs are also powerful greenhouse gases, each molecule being 10,000 times more powerful than carbon dioxide. CFCs are a fraction of the emissions of carbon dioxide but nevertheless it is estimated that, unless the Montreal Protocol is strengthened, CFCs will account for 13 per cent of global warming by 2030.

In the foam plastics industry, a number of manufacturers aim to reduce the amount of CFC used in foam blowing by 50 per cent by the end of 1990. Packaging for egg boxes, meat trays and fast food can be made with other fibres and plastics, and reduce by 100 per cent the CFCs used in this area. Natural fibres and latex rubber are two alternatives that can be used in furniture. Improvements must also be made in the manufacturing process, as a high proportion of CFCs escape during production.

The biggest problem in the refrigeration and air conditioning sector is leakage of CFCs from joints and seals. Estimates from the USA suggest that one third of CFC 12 used in air conditioning is lost because of leakage. To date, manufacturers and retailers have done very little about organising safe disposal of fridges and air conditioning systems at the end of their useful lives. Some local authorities are arranging for pick-ups, but it is still a very hit and miss affair.

ICI of Britain and Du Pont of America are developing a chlorine-free replacement for CFC 12 in air conditioners and refrigerators. ICI is due to open a manufacturing plant in Runcorn in 1991, and Du Pont is building a plant in Texas to produce the new alternative in 1991. Fourteen different CFC producers are putting together an evaluation of alternatives and their effect on the environment. The final report, due in mid-1990, will include studies on the effects to stratospheric ozone, tropospheric ozone, global warming and acid deposition.

Percentage of ozone removed by chlorinated substances based on 1985 emissions

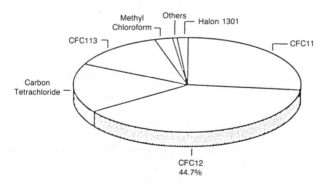

Source: Stratospheric Ozone Review Group

Meanwhile the chlorine builds up in the stratosphere, and the 'hole' over the Antarctic continues to grow. The preservation of the ozone layer is in the hands of worldwide governments and market forces. Hopefully, decisive action, not prevarication, will be forthcoming from both sides. On this particular issue, the evidence of over 30 years' research is before them and there is no lack of evidence to hide behind. Eminent scientists are clamouring for an outright ban on all chlorine substances. Profits don't come into it; unless the ozone layer is saved, we'll be in for a roasting.

Take Action
You
— do not buy furniture filled with polyurethane foam that has been treated with CFCs
— check that the insulation installed in your house is CFC free
— if you are going to buy a new fridge, check out what refrigerant and form of insulation it uses. HCFC22 is not perfect but is a lot better than CFC 11 and 12. Do this by contacting the manufacturer
— if you have air conditioning in your car, home or office, make sure there are no leaks and keep it well maintained
— if you want to dispose of an old fridge or air conditioning system, liaise with the local authority to arrange collection and safe recycling of the CFCs. If this service is not available press the council and local retailers to provide facilities for recycling. It's expensive but worth it in the long run.
The Government
— introduce an all-embracing 'ozone friendly' labelling system so that consumers know exactly what they are buying
— demand a total phase-out of CFCs, halons and other substances harmful to the ozone layer by 1995
— fund and organise CFC recycling units around the country for old fridges, commercial refrigeration systems and air conditioning systems
— ensure that CFC production standards are less wasteful
— ensure that further help is given to developing countries who will greatly benefit from new 'ozone friendly' technology
Safer alternatives: HFC 125, HFC 134a, HFC 143a, HFC 152a.

Chapter 5

Vehicles and Transport

The last two years have seen a growth in awareness of many environmental issues, but none so obvious as the campaign to reduce harmful vehicle emissions, in particular lead. The UK has over 22 million cars, buses and lorries on the roads, driving over 300 billion kilometres a year. As a result, the environment is being gradually eroded: vehicle emissions pollute the air, road networks destroy the countryside, and noise and congestion put pressure on our cities, not to mention the dangers excess vehicles present to people, in particular children. The Government has made moves to encourage owners of vehicles to adopt cleaner fuel, but action is slow. Environmentalists now say that a completely new transport policy is essential to curb the effects vehicles are having on our planet.

> *Every year the total amount of pollutants emitted by vehicles in the UK would fill a tunnel 10 metres wide and long enough to encircle the earth.*

Lead in petrol

It has been known since the 1970s that the vehicles which have dramatically increased our mobility in the last 50 years have also constituted a grave danger. Research studies demonstrated back in the 1970s the fact that exhaust emissions contained dangerous toxins, in particular lead. Later, in the 1980s, conclusive evidence pointed to the fact that lead in the environment was affecting children's development. A study published in *The Lancet* in 1987 demonstrated that children with higher lead levels in their blood performed less well intellectually than those with lower levels, and particularly in tests of number skills and reading ability. Later, four major studies showed that lead exposure in pregnancy affects foetal development. Studies from the USA, Australia and the UK demonstrated a highly significant relationship between foetal exposure to lead and birth weight, head circumference and development during the first two years of life. All subjects used in these studies were leading normal life-styles; the vast majority of them had levels of lead well within the normal range. Scientists carrying out the research concluded that no child born into the modern world can be considered immune from the effects of low-level lead exposure.

> *Lead is a poison. It is potentially damaging to childrens' health and development.*
> Virginia Bottomley, Junior Environment Minister, 1989.

Another key point which emphasises the dangers of lead is the fact that it is non-degradable, i.e. it remains forever in the atmosphere. Consequently, this year's lead pollution will add to that of all previous years so that its environmental presence increases all the time. The longer we continue to pump lead into the atmosphere, the more it will accumulate. From the results of medical evidence it is blatantly obvious that lead in the atmosphere must be reduced.

In 1981 a leaked memo from the Chief Medical Officer at the DHSS warned of the dangers to young children's intelligence posed by lead in petrol, and in 1983 a Royal Commission on Environmental Pollution published a strong recommendation that immediate action should be taken to remove lead from petrol. For once, this was an environmental health problem that could be tackled relatively easily. Petrol does not naturally contain lead, and it is added in order to prevent 'knocking' (to ensure that petrol burns rather than explodes); it is also added to lubricate the car's engine valves. The answer was to build cars which did not need such lubrication and to stop adding lead to petrol.

In 1981 CLEAR, the Campaign for Lead Free Air, started putting pressure on the Government and the motor and petroleum industries to provide the facilities and incentives for the British public to drive on unleaded fuel. This meant ensuring an adequate supply of unleaded fuel in garages, providing information on how to have cars adjusted to run on unleaded, and a financial incentive for the public to make the change.

Despite such pressure, and despite the evidence of the dangers of lead to children and unborn babies, it was not until an EEC Directive of 1985 stated that member countries must make unleaded petrol widely available by October 1989 that CLEAR's proposals were followed up. In the March budget of 1989, the Chancellor introduced a 10p price differential between leaded and unleaded petrol, a move which the Motor Agents Association calculated could constitute a saving of around £30 a year for the average motorist driving 9,400 miles. This saving would easily cover the cost of adjusting cars which cannot already run on unleaded petrol.

The budget provided the financial incentive, but much confusion still abounds over the use of unleaded petrol. This is reflected in drivers' resistance to take advantage of the price differential. CLEAR estimates that there are already four million cars in Britain which could run on unleaded petrol without adjustment, and a further nine million could do so with minor adjustment. That means 13 million cars, more than half the total in Britain, could easily be running on unleaded fuel now, yet sales of unleaded six months after the budget still only amounted to 20 per cent of total fuel revenue.

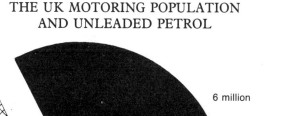

THE UK MOTORING POPULATION
AND UNLEADED PETROL

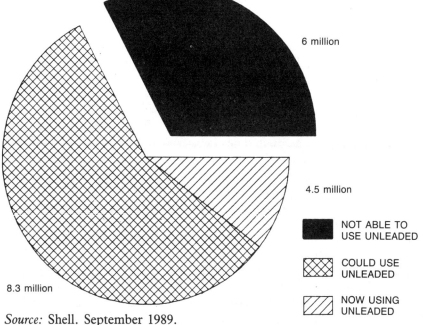

6 million

4.5 million

■ NOT ABLE TO
USE UNLEADED

▨ COULD USE
UNLEADED

▨ NOW USING
UNLEADED

8.3 million

Source: Shell. September 1989.

Other European countries are strides ahead in the battle to beat lead. When sales of unleaded were only 16 per cent of all fuel revenue in Britain, Germany was leading the field with a figure of 53 per cent; in Denmark the percentage was 34 and in Norway 27. Europe as a whole lags way behind the USA, where only unleaded fuel is sold and all cars run on it.

Despite a significant price incentive in Britain and wide availability in garages, even now the low rate of consumption reflects the confusion surrounding the issue. If you drive a car and do not already use unleaded petrol, the guidelines below will indicate how to adjust and make the change towards cheaper motoring and a cleaner and healthier environment.

Questions answered

★ How do I know if my car can take unleaded or not?

Many new models of cars can already run on unleaded petrol without any adjustment. After 1990, by law all new cars will have the facility to run on unleaded. Your present vehicle will fall into one of three categories as far as petrol is concerned.

— it will run on unleaded petrol with no adjustment
— it can be modified to run on unleaded petrol
— it will not run on unleaded and cannot be modified

To find out which category your car fits into, ring a franchised dealer or agent for your particular vehicle. Ask for the service department. State the model, engine type, year and series of your car. The garage will inform you which category of car you have and, if it needs adjustment, where this can be done and how much it will cost.

★ If my car is adjusted to take unleaded, can I still fill up with leaded? A car converted to unleaded petrol can also run on leaded with no risk of damaging the engine. If, however, your car has been fitted with a catalytic converter (see below) you can only fill up with unleaded.

★ What will it cost to adjust my car to unleaded petrol? Some garages will adjust your car free of charge when it has its next service. The Society of Motor Manufacturers and Traders states that conversion costs between £5 and £35, depending on the make and registration of your car. Even if it costs you £35, the price differential on leaded petrol will virtually allow you to recoup the cost of adjustment within one year.

★ How will unleaded fuel affect the performance of my car? If your car is suitable, or has been adjusted to unleaded, you will notice no significant reduction in performance.

★ Some people say that once the car is adjusted I should alternate between leaded and unleaded petrol? In the case of some engines which have been adjusted to take unleaded fuel, you may be advised to fill up with one tank of leaded to every three of unleaded fuel. This is because the type of metal used in the engine valves can still benefit from the periodic use of lead to provide lubrication. Your dealer should tell you if this is necessary.

★ What about other machines using petrol fuel? Most motorbikes and petrol-driven machines should be able to run on unleaded fuel, but it is advisable to consult the manufacturer or dealer for accurate advice on the individual product.

If you are unable to get adequate information about running your car on unleaded fuel from your dealer or local garage phone these help lines:

★ CLEAR 01-387 4970
★ AA 0836 401525
★ RAC 021 430 7392

In the majority of cases, switching to unleaded petrol is an easy option. Unleaded petrol is now widely available and it makes sense environmentally and financially to take this easy opportunity to clean up the atmosphere, and make our cities safer places for our children.

Other pollutants in petrol
But unfortunately lead is not the only danger lurking in our car exhausts.

Vehicles emit a wide range of chemical substances, many of them harmless, but three of which are dangerous pollutants released in sufficient amounts to affect human health and have serious implications on the environment. The pollutants which cause the most concern are carbon monoxide, hydrocarbons and nitrogen oxides.

Car exhaust fumes adding CO_2, CO and nitrous oxides to the atmosphere.

Carbon monoxide

Carbon monoxide is a poisonous gas which, when inhaled, limits the body's capacity to absorb oxygen. As we know, if you shut yourself in a garage with no ventilation and leave the engine running, you will eventually stop breathing. Dense exhaust fumes in the atmosphere have the same effect, be it more gradual, succeeding in limiting oxygen supplies to the body, which in turn puts greater strain on the heart. The World Health Organisation has published guidelines for safe emissions of carbon monoxide. These are regularly exceeded in London.

> *An average car emits five lungfuls of poisonous carbon monoxide gas per mile.*

Carbon monoxide is also a powerful greenhouse gas. Cars and light vans contribute to 18 per cent of the carbon emissions which thicken the protective layer of gases around the Earth contributing to global warming (see Chapter 1).

Hydrocarbons

Hundreds of different types of hydrocarbons are emitted from vehicle exhausts. The long-term inhalation of such gases is harmful to health and, although no acceptable exposure level has been submitted, studies have shown that breathing in hydrocarbons increases the risk of lung cancer. Hydrocarbons also contribute both to acid rain and to ozone formation.

Nitrogen oxide

Forty per cent of nitrogen oxide emissions in Britain come from vehicles. Driving at speeds over 50mph greatly increases their production. The main problem with nitrogen oxide is that it contributes to forms of photochemical pollution such as ozone, which in high levels can cause eye, nose and throat irritation and affect the respiratory system attacking the lungs. People with cardiac and respiratory weaknesses, children, asthmatics and those suffering with bronchitis are particularly susceptible.

Another danger of the release of nitrous oxides is their contribution to acid rain, the chemical cocktail which can attack lakes, forests, ancient buildings etc (see Chapter 3).

So, even if we take the relatively easy step of opting for unleaded petrol, our cars are still polluting the planet and damaging our health. What is the answer?

Catalytic converters

Again, the solution is not so difficult. Some 20 years ago, the Americans became aware of the fact that poisonous vehicle emissions could be rendered virtually harmless by attaching a contraption known as a catalytic converter to the exhaust. The device comprises a steel casing within which a ceramic or metal support is coated with a catalyst of precious metals. The catalytic converter chemically converts at least 90 per cent of carbon monoxide, nitrogen oxides and hydrogen emissions into water, nitrogen and carbon dioxide. Catalytic converters are poisoned and damaged by leaded petrol; attaching them to cars forces drivers to run only on unleaded fuel, an added bonus.

For 15 years it has been illegal in the USA to produce a new car without a three-way catalytic converter. Emissions have drastically been cut as a consequence. Over the last ten years, Japan, Australia, Switzerland, Austria and Sweden have introduced similar legislation.

Ironically, the world's leading catalyst manufacturer is British. Yet, despite the company's success abroad, business at home has been very slow. The British car manufacturing industry has been very reluctant to catch up with the clean technology being offered and vehemently resisted pressure to adopt catalytic converters for many years, advocating instead an alternative technology known as the 'lean burn engine'. This system operates by increasing the amount of air mixed with petrol so that less fuel is burnt (a financial incentive) and, under ideal conditions, exhaust emissions are reduced. However, trials have shown that the lowering of emissions is only achieved when a car is cruising. At full throttle, the engine must burn a richer mixture of petrol to air and emissions immediately rise exceeding the US legislation.

Catalytic converters have been proved to reduce air pollution by 75 per cent.

One of the arguments that the motor industry presented against catalytic converters was the fact that cars fitted with them do consume marginally more fuel, which raises expenditure and is ecologically unsound. However, catalysts have been proved to reduce air pollution by 75 per cent at any speed, and consequently the car industry has had to back down as EEC legislation has pushed for their adoption in member states. From 1992, all new cars must come up to USA standards for emissions; this means that all new cars will have to be fitted with catalytic converters and subsequently will run only on unleaded petrol.

So much for the new cars. What about the old ones most of us are still driving? Some manufacturers are already offering to retrofit old models with catalytic converters. Volkswagen, for example will fit them on all post-1979 models of VW and Audi. However, the main drawback to the consumer is the cost. While catalytic converters may cost the manufacturer around £50 to buy, to fit them requires skilled labour and may well bump up the price of a new car by between £100 and £1000 depending on the model. Volvo, however, is now offering to fit catalytic converters free on all newly-bought models.

> *If the UK Government is serious about stopping the greenhouse effect it should stop wasting time on long-term impracticalities such as nuclear power and look at what can be achieved now.*
>
> Greenpeace Spokesperson on the subject of catalytic converters, 1989.

In an attempt to encourage drivers to opt for cars with converters, or to have them fitted on older models, some European countries are offering tax incentives. West Germany and Greece, for example, offer a discount on road tax dependent on reduction of exhaust emission. Denmark and Holland are considering similar schemes.

A green transport policy

Using unleaded petrol and fitting catalytic converters will dramatically reduce the levels of pollution caused by vehicle emissions. But, despite the technology, cars will still continue to be one of the principal contributors to air pollution. Catalysts convert carbon monoxide into carbon dioxide, which is less toxic, but equally polluting to the environment. What is needed, say environmentalists, is a complete rethink of transport policy which will look at the long-term effects of transport, not just the short-term solutions. A policy which will consider not only air pollution, but problems such as energy efficiency, safety, noise, the implication of different systems of transport on cities and the countryside and ultimately society at large, to establish which are the most environmentally sound and economically efficient methods of moving from A to B for the sake of both humans and the planet.

A transport policy which advocates private cars is not a policy which protects the environment. Quite apart from the question of air pollution, individual cars are avid consumers of valuable energy sources which will not last forever. The following table shows how many litres of petrol per 100 passenger kilometres different modes of transport consume.

Private	*(Fuel expenditure per 100 passengers)*
car commuting	9.2
off-peak car	4.2
motor cycle	5.0
moped	2.1
Public	
taxi	12.2
commuting bus	1.4
off-peak bus	2.8
minibus	2.2
express coach	0.9
high speed train	2.0
aircraft	9.0

(*Energy and personal travel*, Hillman and Whalley)

From the table we see that cars and taxis exceed aircraft in terms of fuel expenditure per hundred passengers and are by far the least efficient of the land-based modes of transport. Given that pollution levels relate to fuel consumption, private cars and taxis are also the greatest polluters.

Air pollution and energy conservation aside, private vehicles also come under attack when we consider rural and urban environments. Current levels of traffic seriously undermine the quality of life in our cities. Noise and danger resulting from too many vehicles has played a significant role in making inner cities unpleasant places to be.

At peak time averages, one bus carries the occupants of 22 cars

Source: Friends of the Earth

Surveys in the 1970s showed that 40 per cent of Britain's urban population suffered from traffic-induced noise. Added to this is the vibration caused by heavy goods vehicles and the annoyance of air traffic suffered by all city dwellers.

In the last ten years, 62,000 people have been killed on Britain's roads, 800,000 people have been seriously injured, and 2,500,000 have been slightly injured. A situation exists where citizens have to alter their behaviour to ensure their safety; children cannot walk to school, it is too dangerous to ride a bicycle, and the elderly or disabled cannot cross the road quickly enough.

Then there are the implications that an excessive number of cars have on society's infrastructure. Roads can not only ruin the countryside, but also divide communities. Because cars take up room, they have the overall effect of spreading people out and making them more insular — driving to a distant supermarket in your car is a different experience to walking to the local shops, where you may meet other members of the community on the way.

The answer is, of course, to reduce the number of private motor vehicles. But to do this there must be viable, efficient and economic alternatives, either pleasant and safe facilities in which to walk or cycle, or reliable modes of public transport.

A traffic jam in Swansea. Not an unfamiliar sight to city dwellers!

Providing for pedestrians must be a top priority for any environmentally-conscious government. Surveys show that an overwhelming proportion of the journeys people use cars for could easily be done on foot or by bicycle. The problem is that roads and pavements are often too busy, noisy or polluted to make walking a pleasant alternative to driving. Reallocation of space within the structure of roads is necessary to allow for wider pavements, and greater emphasis should be placed on creating pedestrianised areas.

A similar programme is needed for cyclists. Statistics show that far more people are able to ride bicycles than drive cars, yet are put off doing so by the dangers of urban traffic. Cycling has been ignored in transport planning for years. Even today, little effort is made to cater for the ever-growing demand for safe cycling routes. Environmental groups are campaigning for more money and importance to be placed on the needs of cyclists, with a target of doubling cycle use over the next five years.

The greatest incentive, however, to reduce car use is to provide an efficient and popular public transport service. In many European cities, and more recently in the USA, it has been accepted that the only efficient and cost effective way of moving people in and out of cities is by rail. In Britain delays, strikes and overcrowding on trains make this public service an undesirable option. Environmentalists call for priority to be given to provide a frequent, reliable and cheap railway and tube network which will encourage more people to leave their cars at home.

Changing modes of transport in some European capitals

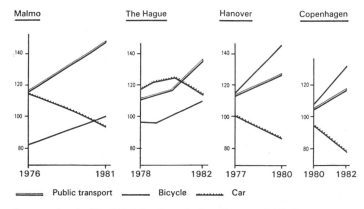

Source: Apel, D. 1984 Stadtverkehrsplanugn Teil 3

Proportion of public transport costs met by sudsidy — 1984/5	City	Percentage
	Turin	87
	Rome	81
	Rotterdam	81
	Amsterdam	80
	Genoa	79
	Sheffield	78
	Seattle	70
	Athens	70
	Bordeaux	70
	Miami	69
	Los Angeles	69
	Antwerp	66
	Stockholm	63
	Milan	62
	Paris	54
	London	30

Source: Jane's Urban Transport Systems, 1985

Take Action
If you own a car
— switch to unleaded
— approach your dealer to ask if your car can be fitted with a catalytic converter
— when buying a new model opt for a smaller vehicle which consumes less fuel and make sure it has a catalytic converter fitted
When you drive
— think before doing so — do you really need to take the car?
— try to share lifts with others
— drive slowly — it's safer and it consumes less fuel; avoid sudden stops and use the gears to slow down rather than making sudden brake stops
Use alternative methods of transport
— walk more often
— invest in a bicycle
— support public transport
— campaign with your local council to improve public transport facilities in your area.

Chapter 6

Rainforests

Beady eyes glimmer through the foliage, now and again bright shafts of sunlight penetrate the thick green canopy and hundreds of flowers turn their heads towards the source. Hot and steamy, the smell of moist decay pervades the air. Trees 160 feet high thrust their crowns above the canopy, their trunks buttressed by strange outgrowths, and clothed in exotic plants. Traditional tribespeople live their whole lives in this rich, green cocoon, gathering food and medicines and sharing their habitat with the weird and the wonderful.

View over the canopy of palm leaves in the Vallée de Mai, Seychelles.

The rainforests are some of the most magical regions on the Earth, full of life and promise. Half the animal species of the world and 90,000 out of 250,000 known plant species, live in the rainforests. Yet the rainforests cover just seven per cent of global landmass. They are regions of huge biological diversity, a treasure chest of invaluable worth, representing 60 million years of evolution.

One in four products from the chemist will contain chemical compounds derived from rainforest plants, and it is estimated that to date only one per cent of rainforest plants have been screened for medical use. The ones that have provide the basis for antibiotics, the Pill, dental cement, tranquillisers, heart and ulcer drugs.

Some medical uses of tropical rainforest plants

Malaria — effectively treated with quinine, from the cinchona tree of Peru

Surgery — much relies on d-turbocurarine, a muscle relaxant made from curare which comes from an Amazonian liana

Amoebic dysentry — since the time of Louis XIV it has been treated with ipecac, a South American plant

Birth control — diosgenin from Mexican and Guatemalan wild yams is a major component of the contraceptive pill

Hypertension — often treated with resperine, from the SE Asian shrub *Rauwolfia serpentina*

Schizophrenia — schizophrenic convulsions are relieved by picrotoxin from the Levan berry of S. and S. E. Asia. It is also used to restore breathing following a barbiturate overdose

Dental cement — comes from balsams of Latin America

Glaucoma — treated with diosgenin from the West African calabar bean

Antiseptic — the benzoin tree of Malaysia yields a substance used both as an antiseptic and against bronchitis

Source: World Wide Fund for Nature

The US National Cancer Institute has identified 3,000 plants with anti-cancer properties, 70 per cent of which originate in the rainforests. Already the rosy periwinkle from Madagascar has made a major contribution to curing child-hood leukaemia and other blood cancers. The survival rate has gone up from 20 per cent in 1960 to 80 per cent now.

Many foods are also descended from tropical forest plants, among them rice, maize, coffee, tea, pineapples, peanuts, aubergines, bananas, oranges and lemons, mangoes and papaya. Future foods may come from leaf protein, the winged bean (the tropic's answer to the soybean) and dozens of fruits includ-ing the pummelo (a large citrus fruit from Southeast Asia), the soursop from South America and the mangosteen from Malaysia. The serendipity berry from West Africa is 3,000 times as sweet as sugar and doesn't rot your teeth!

In 1985 the World Bank listed important by-products of the tropical forests and included the following:

essential oils	dyestuffs
waxes	pesticides
edible oils	gum
Brazil nuts	latex
rattan	resins
bamboo	tannins
spices	

These are all products which are taken from the forests without harming them — in other words, sustainable use.

Tragically, this type of use has been overtaken by non-sustainable exploitation, where massive tracts of rainforest are wiped off the face of the earth for logs, cattle grazing, mining and construction development. In ten minutes, a tree hundreds of years old that supports many other plant and animal lives can be destroyed with the snick of a chainsaw. In a day, several acres of rainforest can be burned down by ranchers to make space for hungry cattle.

Decline of the rainforests

Each year 200,000 sq kms of rainforest are ripped out worldwide and, at present levels, scientists estimate that the tropical rainforests will be just a memory by the year 2050. Before the wanton destruction began there were 16 million sq kms of rainforest around the world; that figure has been halved since the end of the Second World War.

Annual losses of rainforests around the world

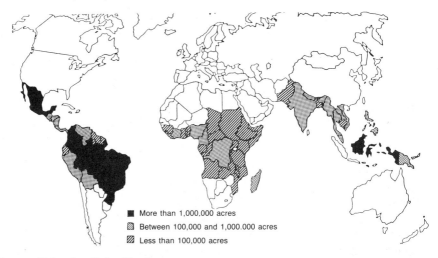

■ More than 1,000,000 acres
▨ Between 100,000 and 1,000,000 acres
▨ Less than 100,000 acres

Source: Friends of the Earth

Burning of rainforest trees is believed to release between 15 and 25 per cent of all carbon dioxide into the atmosphere, and is therefore a substantial contribution to the greenhouse effect. Depletion of the rainforests can also have other climatic effects, such as altering air and temperature patterns. Deforestation results in the already poor soil becoming virtually infertile, due to loss of topsoil.

The Ivory Coast is a fearful example of what can result from full scale exploitation. Over the last 20 years the country has lost 90 per cent of its original 15 million hectares of forest. The forests have been extensively logged and then cleared for cocoa, coffee, rubber and palm oil crops. The implications of treeless and desiccated soil are very bad for agriculture. One study carried out in the region showed that a forested slope lost 0.03 tons of soil per hectare per year, whereas a deforested slope lost 138 tons a landslide.

The great floods that occurred in Thailand in November 1988 cost many lives and alerted the government to the serious effect of cutting down rainforest. The scale of the damage was in part due to deforestation in the area, which meant that the torrential rain was not absorbed by trees and vegetation. Twenty years ago the rainforests covered 65 per cent of Thailand, now they only cover 12 per cent.

Two thirds of Brazilian Amazonia (3.8 million sq kms) have been designated for development by the end of this century. The Brazilian government plans to build more roads into the heart of the rainforest for developers to prospect for oil and metals. The Amazonian rainforests make up one third of all rainforests and are vitally important in terms of biological diversity.

In 1987 200,000 sq kms of Amazonia were destroyed and two dams, the Tucuri and Balbina, flooded around 4,500 sq kms of rainforest. Many animals and plants are at risk, together with people, and, in Brazil, pressure is mounting from the indigenous tribes such as the Kayapo, and from the rubber tappers union, to bring a halt to the destruction that is ruining their livelihoods.

Tropical rainforests occur in several parts of the world, mostly in developing countries:

— South America has the largest concentration of rainforest including Brazil, Equador, Paraguay, Colombia, Peru, Guyana, Surinam and Costa Rica.

— West Africa also has a significant proportion in the countries of the Ivory Coast, Nigeria, the Congo, Gabon, Zaire, Cameroon and Madagascar.

— Southeast Asia has extensive rainforests in Papua New Guinea, Thailand, Vietnam, Indonesia, Burma, Malaysia, the Philippines and India.

— North West Australia also has rainforest.

All these countries have been affected in one way or another by escalating destruction.

What are rainforests?

Rainforests occur in and around the equator and, as such, have constant sunshine beating down all year round, providing temperatures of between 64°F and 86°F. In addition to extreme warmth, the rainforests also need lots of moisture. There are many different types of tropical forest, but leading rainforest expert, Dr Norman Myers, has attempted to classify a 'true' rainforest. He lists several common characteristics:

1) A rainforest receives at least 4,000mm of rain every year, 200mm of it falling each month for ten months.
2) The wettest of the rainforests have 200mm falling every month.
3) The rainforest is a self-supporting ecosystem with an abundance of trees and vegetation.
4) It has a thick canopy of tree tops often 20 feet thick and a sub canopy of younger trees reaching for the light. The largest trees, known as 'emergents' tower above the top canopy.
5) The richest rainforests can support up to 1,000 tonnes in weight of plants and trees per hectare.

Within these broad terms, there are two separate categories of rainforests. 'Primary' rainforest is an area that hasn't been disturbed for hundreds of years and has reached a state of mature complexity; it is also known as virgin forest. Some scientists believe that it can take up to a thousand years for virgin forest to be truly established. If a primary forest is cleared and the ground left to its own devices, a young forest will begin to grow. This is known as 'secondary' forest. The secondary forest is much less diverse, trees may not last so long, more sunshine reaches the ground and different plants grow. But eventually, without disturbance, the secondary forest will reach such a state of maturity to be classified as primary.

Contrary to popular belief, rainforests are not jungles through which you have to slash a path; the tree tops screen out much of the sun and ground level plants do not grow that abundantly providing room to walk around in. The soil on which rainforests grow is generally very poor but despite this, rainforests flourish because of the heat and the rain and the continual decay of vegetation that occurs on the ground.

One of the most important functions of a rainforest is its role in the rain cycle. The tree roots act like a giant sponge when the rain falls, drawing up water from the ground which is then given off as vapour through the leaves. The rainforest also plays a key role in good irrigation. The thick canopy of leaves and branches disperse the rainwater so that it falls on the ground softly and evenly, avoiding floods. As the water trickles down into the water table, the rivers receive a constant supply of water and can irrigate agricultural land effectively.

> *There's no reason why people shouldn't use their rainforests, but it's on what basis that counts. It's silly to say 'stop immediately' — they can't, it's like Britain stopping to fish.*   Claire Birch, Living Earth

If rainforests are cut down or semi-destroyed, the ecological effect on the surrounding land can be disastrous. Without the regulation of the rainforests, rivers become swollen or parched with dire effects on fragile crops. The all-important top soil quickly disappears, and leaches into the rivers, making the water muddy brown and scuppering any chance of a new forest growing up. Without the protection of the trees to bind soil and act as a windbreak, the land can be fiercely lashed by landslides, earthquakes and storms.

Virgin rainforests are astonishingly rich in tree and plant species. In the countries of Brunei and Sarawak, Southeast Asia, there are 2,500 native tree species in an area of only 126,000 sq kms. In comparison, the UK has only 35 native species in 244,000 sq km. Each rainforest tree supports many other plants and it is not uncommon to discover 30 different species on one tree including ferns, vines and orchids.

The tropical rainforests of Equador in South America contain between 15,000 and 20,000 plant species, whereas the whole of Europe has only 13,000. The Choco region of Colombia has one of the richest floras anywhere in the world — in one tenth of a hectare, 208 tree species have been found. Compare that to a whole forest in the UK that may contain just a few species.

The animal life is also very rich. Southeast Asia is home to 656 mammals, 850 amphibians and 700 butterflies. In the Tambotata Reserve, Peru, there can be found 530 bird species compared to 850 in the USA and Canada combined. Anteaters, sloths, armadillos, hummingbirds, macaws, bats, orang-utans, lots of strange 'flying' animals including frogs, squirrels and geckos all live in the rainforest. As do many insects, spiders, beetles, ants, butterflies and moths.

When you understand the complexity and the long-lived nature of the rainforests, you can begin to appreciate the size of the tragedy that is unfolding. Most of the rainforests belong to developing countries which have to resort to milking their most precious resource to make ends meet, and to pay back money lent to them by Western countries.

Struggle for survival

Over the last two decades, the World Bank, the International Monetary Fund and various other organisations have lent developing countries huge amounts of money, on which the interest alone is staggering. The situation is hopeless and, to pay back just the interest, countries have to scrimp and save every penny; that means no proper forest protection and leaving forests in the hands of the merchants, often unscrupulous and owned by foreign companies. This has the short-term effect of bringing in foreign currency.

The fact that most of the rainforest is uninhabited, with only a few pockets of indigenous communities, makes exploitation attractive. Governments turn a blind eye to the thousands of poverty-stricken families that migrate to the forest every year. These are usually landless people who have no hope of anything except scratching a living in the forest. Unlike the indigenous tribes, they often have little or no agricultural know-how and simply slash and burn the forest as they go. The soil is capable of producing a couple of crops before becoming infertile when the mobile homeless move on.

It has been estimated that these subsistence farmers are globally responsible for half of all rainforest destruction, as they march deeper and deeper into virgin forest. Any kind of ranching, logging or building provides a ready-made inroad for the farmers to penetrate the most inaccessible parts.

In contrast, the indigenous peoples have a much more realistic approach to agriculture. They grow 'gardens' of all kinds of produce; the plants are chosen to complement one another and ward off insect and fungi attacks. A typical garden would contain fruit and vegetables, a few chickens to scratch around, bushes for firewood, medicinal plants, rubber trees, plants for animal feed, spices, and bamboo for building. And all that on only a couple of acres.

But for the last twenty years, and increasingly so at the moment, quick profits are what the rainforests are all about. The Western world provides a willing market for forest products, particularly hardwoods and beef cattle. The trade in tropical hardwoods has already peaked and stocks in some countries are rapidly running down. Mahogany was once prolific in the tropical forests, and having logged out the Caribbean and West Africa, merchants are now moving back to Brazil.

The logging of timber is estimated to destroy or damage 12.5 million acres of tropical forests every year. The main timber-exporting regions are Southeast Asia and West Africa. Nigeria's rainforests have been so exploited for logs that the country now imports more hardwood than it exports. Hardwood stocks in the Ivory Coast, Malaysia and the Philippines have also been severely depleted.

Logging of trees in tropical rain forest, Philippines.

The biggest problem is that loggers do not replace the felled trees with new saplings; the option of creating plantations is largely ignored. Instead, virgin forest is plundered, and behind the loggers come thousands of displaced migrant farmers who destroy any chance the land may have had of regenerating itself.

Main consumers

Europe and Japan are the largest Western markets for tropical hardwoods and import between 12 and 15 million cubic tonnes of timber a year. At the moment the export of ready-made furniture is subject to a tariff on its entrance to the EEC, whereas raw logs are not. This encourages logging companies to send over plain logs, but it would be more profitable if the countries themselves designed and built furniture and fitments and sold it direct to the West.

Hardwoods are remarkably tough and long lasting — that's why they're so popular. Eighty per cent of tropical hardwoods are made into furniture. Next time you think about it, have a look round your home, — you might notice the hardwood veneer on the TV set, kitchen cupboards, parquet flooring, doors, window frames, shelves and tables. They could all be made from tropical hardwoods such as teak, mahogany, ramin, meranti or luan.

The UK is the biggest consumer of tropical hardwoods after Japan, and 99 per cent of our supplies come from unsustainable sources, in other words forest that is gone for ever once the loggers have moved in. It has been calculated by scientists that, for every tree felled in the rainforests, ten others will die or be wounded by knock-on effects. In the unique structure of the rainforest, creepers interweave between branches and can either tear a neighbouring tree down or rip out branches, leaving it vulnerable to disease.

South America, on the other hand, has suffered greatly at the hands of the cattle ranchers. The majority of the beef raised is sold to satisfy the enormous appetite of the USA. Most of the beef exported ends up as hamburgers, pet food, processed meats and baby foods. The demand for cheap beef arose when North American beef soared in price, — cattle ranching in South America is far less costly and a lucrative business deal for wealthy landowners.

In Central America, more than a quarter of the rainforest has been converted to grass for grazing, and Costa Rica has lost one third of its rainforest to cattle ranchers. The cattle ranching option is popular because the outgoings are low. The virgin forest which is hacked down to make way for the cattle is virtually free, and when the soil is exhausted the ranchers just move on to another plot. In Brazil, large landowners (who are usually very rich anyway) are given government subsidies to burn down trees so that cattle farms can be set up.

What is being done?

So what, if anything, is being done to halt the seemingly relentless march of rainforest destruction? There are actually quite a few positive steps forward:

for a start, and under intense pressure from environmentalists and scientists, the World Bank has begun to take into account conservation when it is approving projects for funding. In the past, developing countries have fallen into ridiculous debt trying to pay back loans that were made for impractical, ludicrously expensive projects.

Other banks and lending institutions are beginning to realise that Third World countries have very little hope of ever paying back the huge loans they have taken out. The Brady Plan (devised by Nicholas Brady the US Treasury Secretary) suggests that owed money could be reduced, and the remainder made into a more realistic secure loan that would be paid back in time. Several UK banks have already put this philosophy into action and written off bad debts running into several thousand million pounds.

> *Many of these countries are suffering under an enormous burden of debt. Structural adjustment programmes are conditional on countries cutting back on basics like food and education, they cannot afford forest conservation officers.* Simon Counsell, Rainforest campaigner, Friends of the Earth.

The United Nations Environmental Programme (UNEP) initiated a Tropical Forest Action Plan in 1985. The plan aims to pull together all the aid programmes being run around the world so that work is not duplicated. UNEP also organises fair loans from rich donor countries to poor developing nations, and is looking to spend $8 billion in aid over five years. Projects are likely to include reforestation, new plantations of quick growing hard woods, growing crops and trees together, and increasing other sustainable uses of rainforest wealth such as drug screening and fruit harvesting.

Another ray of hope is the International Tropical Timber Organisation (ITTO) which was established in 1986. ITTO represents all the countries involved in buying and selling wood from tropical forests and has a stated aim of conservation. It is also under the wing of the United Nations and could contribute to the reforestation of felled rainforest, so that the land is sustained. The ITTO is in a perfect position to demand from its members better practices, such as felling secondary forest rather than primary, chopping up every part of a felled tree so that it is all used (this is not the case in many areas) and replanting after a section of forest has been cleared.

At the present time, only 0.2 per cent of rainforests are protected as national parks. Encouragement and funding by richer nations could establish more national parks, essential for preserving the many different kinds of forest. Such a policy would have to be in conjunction with better policing of regions by park patrols and resident ecologists.

Forest tribespeople have been fighting back. The Penan of Sarawak, the Batak of the Philippines and the Kayapo of Amazonia have all resisted moves to take their lands, so that the they can hold onto their traditional and successful way of life. In 1987 the Penan people formed a human blockade to stop loggers felling trees in their territories. The blockade held for an amazing eight months before the army broke it up. Different blockades are still being organised and will be until the Penan's rights are recognised.

February 1989 saw a giant step forward for the Amazonian Indians in their fight against the Brazilian government and the World Bank. A massive tribal gathering at Altamira helped to stop a $500 million loan to build hydro-electric dams which would have caused untold environmental damage. Under the leadership of Paulinho Paiakan (Chief of the Kayapo people) the Xavante, the Arara, the Gaviao and the Yanomami stood firm against the might of money and earned their territories a much needed respite. An alternative package is being worked out, but will include environmental projects and energy conservation measures.

> *We are fighting to defend the forest. It is because the forest is what makes us, and what makes our hearts go. Because without the forest we won't be able to breathe and our hearts will stop and we will die.*
> Paulino Paiakan, Kayapo leader on his visit to the UK in 1988.

The World Wide Fund for Nature (WWF), Friends of the Earth (FoE) and Living Earth are all environmental action groups involved in preserving the rainforests as far as possible. Living Earth has launched a three year educational programme in the Cameroon, West Africa, to teach local communities about the value of the forests. WWF has a strong connection with the last remaining rainforest in Nigeria, Oban. As well as campaigning for Oban to be made into a national park, WWF is also working closely with the government to nurture sustainable forest management. They believe it is vital that local communities should be able to use the forest's multitude of products without harming the rainforest infrastructure.

Friends of the Earth groups around the world have been publicising the plight of the rainforest and have had particular success in Brazil, supporting Paulinho Paiakan of the Kayapo and other tribal leaders. The UK division of FoE produces the *Good Wood Guide*, a simple run down of tropical hardwood products and their alternatives for consumers and manufacturers alike, so that all interested parties can be sure of buying hardwood that has come from sustainable sources. The *Good Wood Guide* seal of approval is a voluntary labelling system that manufacturers are encouraged to take on board if they can honestly say that they use wood from sustainable sources — so look for the seal of approval.

In January 1989 Thailand shocked the hardwood industry by introducing a complete ban on logging in all its forests. The pressure for wood is now expected to move to Vietnam and Laos. The Philippines also acted and placed a ban on all hardwood exports — again the industry will look elsewhere for its timber, most prominently Sarawak and Sabah on which there is already great pressure.

Gradually, countries are coming to their senses and realising that non-stop exploitation of rainforest resources is not a long term answer to poverty.

Campaigning groups have served to shine a spotlight on many of the world's diminishing rainforests and are making the guilty West sit up and take note.

Sustainable use is the key idea behind any kind of progress and we must do everything we can to support this, both in terms of financial aid and consumer ethics. It is however up to all of us, developing countries included, to take into account the unique nature of the rainforests and to keep these jewels in the world's crown polished and shining.

Take Action

You
— do not buy tropical hardwood unless it has the *Good Wood Guide* seal of approval — or, better still, don't buy tropical hardwood
— before buying furniture, check whether the wood is tropical hardwood or temperate hardwood
— write to your highstreet bank, most of which are involved in lending large sums to developing countries, and ask them to reconsider their debt-collecting policies

The Government
— take a stance against the amount of tropical hardwoods imported into the UK
— support conservation moves put forward by the International Timber Trade Organisation
— make sure that specific aid to rainforest countries is used to promote sustainable management of resources.

Chapter 7

Waste

Several years ago the British Government boldly declared itself 'conservationist by instinct'. Yet still Britain is nicknamed 'the dustbin of Europe'. Rubbish litters our countryside, toxic fumes are belched into our air and radioactive discharge pollutes our seas. In 1988, while politicians made a show of picking up litter in London parks to encourage public concern, other European countries were several steps ahead in implementing hard-hitting environmental policies. Such issues are now top of the political agenda, and, as 1992 looms, our outraged European partners are putting on pressure for Britain to clean up its environmental act.

Litter disfigures the countryside and contributes to pollution, but this is just the tip of the environmental iceberg. Picking up rubbish and placing it in the bin is one small step in an ever-growing waste crisis. Britain now produces nearly 26 million tons per year of domestic garbage which must be disposed of somewhere, somehow.

The landfill option

Most of this garbage goes to landfill sites — massive holes in the ground where the rubbish is dumped and then covered with clay or top soil. The more domestic rubbish we produce, the more landfill sites are being filled. For the moment, most councils have enough rubbish tips to hold the waste generated in their area. Some, however, have to transport trainloads of rubbish to dumps further afield. London has a major problem in finding room to dispose of all its rubbish. Already 70 per cent of the capital's annual total of 13.5 million tons of waste goes to counties outside the city. In 1986, the London Waste Regulation Authority's annual report stated that London and the commuter belt in the Home Counties would run out of local landfill space well before the end of the century, and counties south and south-west of London would not be able to cope with the burden of the capital's rubbish.

But space availability is not the only problem surrounding the landfill option. Until recently, it was considered safe and environmentally acceptable to dump household waste in the ground where, left to decay, it would break down into harmless by-products and cause no problems. Indeed, it could even serve the purpose of filling quarry sites and aid landscaping. However, several disasters have proved this assumption to be wrong. As household refuse decomposes, it produces an explosive gas, methane, which has been known to seep up through sewage pipes, telephone cables or the top soil covering a site, constituting a serious hazard to nearby buildings.

A scavenging horse at the Tirjohn landfill site, Swansea.

> *In 1985, a girl suffered serious burns following an explosion in a house 50 metres from a landfill in North Yorkshire. The blast happened because a vent to allow gas to escape into the air had become covered over forcing the gas into surrounding rocks.*
> Marek Mayer, The Independent, 1985

An annual report published by HM Inspectorate of Pollution in 1987-88 stated that leakage of methane gas was occurring at around 600 landfill sites situated near buildings in Britain and Wales. Efforts to dump deeper have resulted in even more compacted decaying rubbish and even greater risks. Now authorities are having to monitor landfill sites, a process which is expensive and lengthy.

> *The Department of Environment has confirmed the figure of 1,300 problem waste disposal sites. Of these, 600 need urgent fitting of gas control and most are within 100 yards of houses.*
> Charles Clover, Daily Telegraph

Methane is just one of the problems resulting from dumping rubbish underground. Another is the mixture of toxic liquid seeping out of the decaying rubbish which, with the help of rain falling on the tip, leaches into our groundwater steams. Many landfill sites cater for industrial waste as well as domestic. Therefore, strict monitoring of sites is necessary to prevent these lethal mixtures getting into our water supplies. The more sites there are, the more expensive and difficult adequate monitoring becomes.

Incineration

An alternative method of disposing of waste is to burn it. Some say efficient incineration is preferable to landfill as it can generate heat and electricity. In Denmark, 40 per cent of domestic heating comes from combined heat and power. But there are two major drawbacks. Firstly, new and safe incinerators each cost between £40 and £50 million, a sum which most county councils are unable to afford. And even if the investment were available for in- cinerators of this quality, there is no guarantee that the rate of return from burning waste would recoup the initial outlay and therefore few councils are prepared to take the risk. Consequently, only 6 per cent of UK domestic waste is disposed of through incineration.

The second drawback to incineration is the pollution that it generates. The smoke emitted from the chimneys of incinerators contains a cocktail of chemicals and heavy metals. Plastics, wood and chlorine are just some of the components of waste which, when burnt, generate compounds called diox- ins, extremely toxic substances which are known to cause cancer in animals. Dioxins are deposited on plants and the soil. Once formulated, they remain forever in the environment and build up in food chains and ultimately in our bodies.

While methods can be undertaken to contain the release of toxic fumes, most incinerators presently in use are between 13 and 15 years old and do not meet the pollution safety standards required. Most have been advised to close within the next five years.

Household waste, once thought to be harmless debris, is now recognised as being polluting and hazardous. Most of our refuse does not decompose: plastic containers, bottles and tins dumped in the ground remain forever. When different substances are combined underground or burned, chemicals hazardous to human health can result. The time has come to find a solution to prevent Britain becoming one big, dangerous rubbish tip.

Composition of domestic waste by weight in Europe (1986)

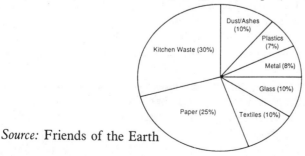

Source: Friends of the Earth

The green alternatives

Recycling is one of the proposed options to solve the waste disposal problem. By separating waste at source, and re-using the materials which can be reprocessed, we will have less waste to dispose of, less land will be needed for landfill and lower levels of pollution will result.

A staggering 70 per cent of Britain's waste comes from packaging alone — plastics, foils, paper and glass — used not only to protect and retain food quality, but also to enhance product appeal, to give them an image which will raise their perceived value. Gone are the days of returnable bottles and jars. Plastic containers, cans and trays line our shop shelves and we have come to expect at least two-fold wrapping and a carrier bag to boot. Such packaging generally uses good quality materials, materials which use up valuable natural resources. Oil is needed to make plastics, for example, bauxite for aluminium cans, and wood for paper.

Our production and disposal of waste threatens valuable resources, as well as polluting the land and the atmosphere. The only solution, therefore, is to reduce the amounts of rubbish we produce. As consumers, there are two ways we can do this:

— choose products which use the minimum of packaging
— choose products which are packaged in materials which can be easily recycled.

The symbol for recycled paper

As consumers we have the power to influence what manufacturers produce. First we can be aware of the unnecessary layers of paper, cardboard and plastic used to make products larger and more glamorous than life, and avoid them. By boycotting products which are overpackaged, you will ultimately change manufacturers' methods of presenting their goods.

A number of products are now packaged in recyclable materials. Glass and paper are the most obvious options. Up to one tenth of our domestic waste is glass, all of which could be recycled without any deterioration in quality. Every tonne of waste glass saves 1.2 tonnes of raw materials and 30 gallons of oil used for processing. Paradoxically, in 1987 we imported 12,000 tonnes of waste glass, while recycling only 13 per cent of the glass we throw away. Britain has only 3,000 bottle banks, that is one for every 17,000 people, compared to Holland, for example, which has one per 1,400 people. In fact Britain recycles the least glass in Europe.

Percentage of glass recycled in Europe	
Switzerland	55%
Holland	53%
Austria	50%
Belgium	50%
Italy	40%
Germany	39%
France	34%
Denmark	27%
Turkey	23%
Spain	23%
Great Britain	15%
Portugal	13%
(British Glass Manufacturers Confederation/Févé)	

Paper could also be easily recycled and would considerably lift the waste disposal burden. The average household throws away 3kg of waste paper every week, most of which ends up in landfill where its breakdown contributes to the production of explosive methane gas. The more paper we produce, the more trees we cut down; 131 million trees are used per year. This means that natural forests or land have to be cleared for wood plantations, which consume large amounts of water and nutrients and give back very little in the way of humus to the soil. Chlorine bleaching of pulp for paper releases dioxins into rivers and soil, further polluting the environment.

A number of the paper products in daily use do not need to be made from virgin paper. Neither do they need to be bleached. Newspapers, toilet paper or tissues are all short life items which could be made from recycled reserves. Moreover, methods now permit recycled paper to have the same aesthetic appeal as virgin pulp. This book is printed on recycled paper. It is perfectly feasible for manufacturers to package their goods in recycled paper without loss of appeal or quality, yet at present only 27 per cent of the paper we consume is recycled, and less than 20 per cent of household newspapers and magazines are recovered.

Wastepaper in the UK

Less than 20% of householders newspapers and magazines are recovered.

Source: Friends of the Earth

Environmentally-conscious consumers should seek to boycott the use of plastics. Although light and convenient, plastic is one of the most environmentally damaging of packaging materials. Plastics constitute 20 per cent by volume of domestic waste in Britain. Most do not degrade. They are bulky and, when placed in landfill sites, remain there forever taking up more and more valuable space each year. When burnt, plastic produces poisonous by-products. Unfortunately, our use of plastics for containers has increased dramatically in the Western World. In 1980, under 10 per cent of drinks bought were in plastic bottles, while in 1987 this figure has risen to nearly 40 per cent.

The technology does exist for recycling plastics but, for it to be successful, packaging would have to be made from one type of plastic only. At present a bottle, for example, can be made from several different types of plastic which would have to be separated out before recycling. Products would have to be clearly labelled to identify the type of plastic they are made from. If reverse vending machines were installed in recycling centres to crush the bottles, sufficient weight of plastic could easily be reclaimed. Unfortunately, however, plastic recycling is little practised in this country although Tesco has set the ball rolling with a limited scheme. The Government could play a part in advocating the recycling of plastics if it were to levy a small charge on each recyclable bottle. This would subsidise collection and recycling costs.

Reclamation of tins presents a similar problem to plastics, owing to the diversity of metals used — tin plate, steel, and aluminium. Aluminium takes a huge amount of energy to produce and is an expensive means of packaging. Consequently, its recycling should take priority.

The US recycles 60 per cent of the 75 billion cans it uses per year. Japan recycles 45 per cent and Australia 50 per cent. Britain recycles only 2 per cent. Various schemes have been set up in Britain to improve this figure. The Save a Can Scheme run by the Can Makers Association provides skips around the country which accept all types of food and drink cans, regardless of size or metal content. However, the number of skips provided is low and there is little incentive for consumers or manufacturers to collect and reprocess. Again, labelling of cans to distinguish which metal they are composed of is essential, as is the imposition of a small levy or resource tax to encourage collection. When we consider that 10 per cent by weight of domestic refuse is metal, and in 1988 a total of 5.6 billion drinks cans were sold in the UK, the need to encourage an efficient and easy recycling scheme is obvious.

So far, Britain has been slow to implement a nationwide recycling programme which will take into account all possible methods of re-using raw materials. The European Community is, however, exerting pressure on member states to make this a priority. It is hoped that, by 1993, European symbols will be marked on consumer goods demonstrating if they are re-usable or can be recycled.

The consumer

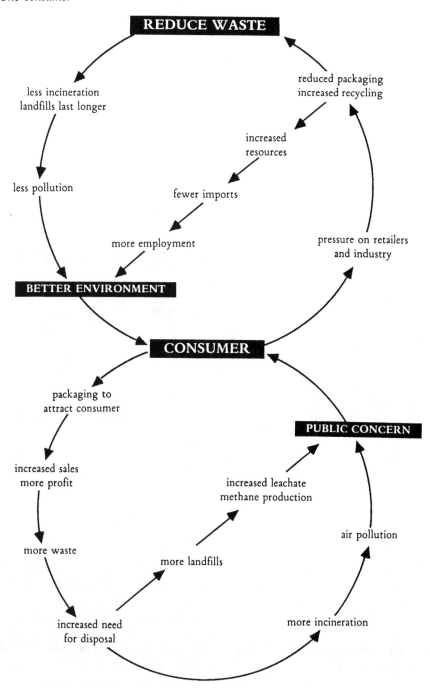

REDUCE WASTE

less incineration
landfills last longer

reduced packaging
increased recycling

increased
resources

less pollution

fewer imports

more employment

pressure on retailers
and industry

BETTER ENVIRONMENT

CONSUMER

packaging to
attract consumer

PUBLIC CONCERN

increased sales
more profit

increased leachate
methane production

air pollution

more waste

more landfills

more waste

more incineration

increased need
for disposal

Source: Friends of the Earth

Hazardous waste

As consumers, we can control domestic refuse. The disposal of industrial and often hazardous waste is another problem, but one with which we should be equally concerned and one which we can ultimately influence.

Around four million tons of industrial waste is disposed of per year in England and Wales. The most common method of disposal is in landfill sites, the second most popular method is dumping it in the ocean, and the rest is incinerated, often in ships at sea.

Part of the problem surrounding the disposal of industrial waste is lack of control. Cases have been reported where dangerous chemicals needing special treatment have been mislabelled and deposited in landfill sites along with domestic refuse. Unless disposed of with great care, landfilling of hazardous waste poses a great threat to the community — the contamination of soil, groundwater and drinking supplies with chemicals dangerous to human health.

A toxic waste dump, Nigeria. *(Friends of the Earth).*

Because disposal of industrial waste is carried out by private enterprise with the sole interest of making a profit, the temptation to dodge intricate and often expensive safety precautions is evident. In 1988 the Government's Hazardous Waste Inspectorate brought to light the fact that, out of 35 landfill sites licensed to receive hazardous waste, only three had laboratory facilities where incoming waste could be analysed. The rest accepted the waste on the basis of the labelling on the containers or its consignment note. In addition, checks by waste disposal authorities are almost impossible to effect, owing to the fact that lorry loads of waste arrive on site every few minutes, are dumped and the tip is covered over at the end of the day. At present, authorities lack the resources to carry out systematic inspections of licensed sites, as there are only 11 officers to cover over 4,000 waste disposal sites in the UK.

As with domestic refuse, the problems of methane gas generation also exist when disposing of industrial waste underground. The Hazardous Waste Inspectorate assessed that 60 per cent of the landfill sites currently active for hazardous waste generated gas in sufficient quantity to warrant careful monitoring.

Not only does Britain have an immense problem coping with its own industrial waste, but it also takes on that of other countries. The amount of industrial waste imported into Britain has multiplied dramatically in the last six years: in 1986/87 some 183,000 tonnes of waste were imported into Britain for treatment or incineration, of which 53,000 were considered to be hazardous. This was a huge increase compared with the 4,000 tonnes imported in 1981. Disposal of waste is big business, and one of the reasons why Britain receives so much is our maintenance of low prices of disposal. It is now cheaper to dump hazardous waste in Britain than it was three years ago, and consequently our imports are still on the increase.

The dumping ground of Europe 1988

130,000 tonnes of industrial waste imported to GB for landfill.
530,000 tonnes of industrial waste imported to GB for treatment or incineration.

Approximate cost of landfill dumping:
France/West Germany: £25 per tonne
Belgium: £25 per tonne
GB: £15 per tonne
(*Source* Friends of the Earth)

The incident of the Karin B, a ship carrying toxic wastes from Europe, illegally imported to Nigeria, which could not find a home and landed up on the south coast of England in the summer of 1987, demonstrated that millions of tonnes of highly toxic waste are being shipped around the globe. As a result of pressure from environmental groups and dock workers, the Karin B did not unload but was sent back to Italy for treatment. However, Third World countries in need of hard currencies are vulnerable to the dumping of toxic waste from the West. Sometimes they are not even informed that the waste is hazardous before it arrives on their doorstep. More than three million tonnes of waste were shipped from the industrialised countries of the South between 1986 and 1988.

The Basle Convention, held in 1989 in an attempt to control such exploitation and to protect developing countries from the industrial debris of the West, did little to help matters. Environmentalists had hoped the Convention would result in enforcing a ban on the export of toxic waste, but the meeting wound up by simply enforcing an obligation of 'notification', whereby the importing country has to be informed of the toxic waste being transferred. The African countries have consequently called for a strong international secretariat to serve as a regulating body in matters of waste disposal.

At Basle, environmentalists also called for stricter regulations on facilities for disposal of toxic waste in importing countries. They stated that adequacy of methods of disposal should at least meet those of the exporting country. But this was opposed by the USA who, having the strictest standards in the world for the disposal of waste, would consequently have been unable to export waste anywhere else. Britain also rejected the proposal, presumably on the grounds that having to bring its standards up to those of the rest of Europe, it would lose out on the lucrative waste disposal trade it presently invites.

Into the sea

While landfill and dumping abroad is not a viable means of disposing of hazardous waste, neither can incineration solve the problem. Britain is the only country in the world which continues to burn hazardous waste at sea. Ninety thousand tonnes of pesticides, solvents, metals and plastics are incinerated per year in burn zones just 100 miles off the British coast. The ships are often without 'scrubbers', the intricate systems which filter toxic fumes before they are released into the atmosphere. These fumes sink from the air onto the top layer of the sea where they are ingested by micro-organisms and accumulate in marine life.

> *The North Sea is the only body of water in the world where the incineration of toxic waste occurs.*
> Greenpeace, 1989

A similar threat to marine life is the discharge of toxic waste into the sea. In many regions, industry is permitted to connect up to the domestic sewage system to discharge its toxic waste. This is then incorporated and becomes an indistinguishable part of the sewage stream. It may escape from sewer leakages or overflows. It may evaporate into the air, or, after passing through the sewage plant, will enter rivers and seas via sewage outflow pipes.

Since the 1950s, radioactive waste from the nuclear reprocessing plant at Sellafield has been discharged directly into the Irish Sea, now thought to be the most radioactive waters in the world. Originally this means of disposal was performed as an experiment to assess what happened to the radioactive material. It was assumed that the liquid discharge would disperse and be rendered harmless. However, active traces carried by currents have been identified as far away as Greenland. Regardless of the effects this waste has on marine life and the fishing industry, it has also been noted that there has been a migration of radioactive material from sea back to coast. The waves breaking on the shore release plutonium, creating a radioactive mist which is then inhaled. Fish from these waters contain levels of radiation higher than in any other waters, and levels of radiation in the atmosphere around Sellafield are higher than around any other nuclear site.

Nuclear waste

Disposal of intermediate level nuclear waste on land also presents a hazard. The industry is now investigating sites in which to dump nuclear waste underground. At Sellafield and Dounreay, drilling is being carried out to assess the suitability of the geological strata of the areas.

Environmentalists oppose the deep burial method for dealing with radio-active waste, claiming that it constitutes a hazard for many thousands of years and should thus be stored above ground where it can easily be monitored for leakages. Any investigations into the suitability of rock formations are, they say, based on assumptions of how that ground will behave now, and do not take into account the possibility of climatic changes, earthquake activity or even human intervention in years to come.

Wherever we live, be it within a stone's throw of Sellafield or in an area seemingly unaffected by the dumping of waste, we must not fall into the out-of-sight, out-of-mind approach adopted by much of industry. The NIMBY (not in my back yard) attitude, whether at home or abroad, does not make for good environmental policy. As landfill sites become gradually more difficult to find, there will soon be no more back yards in which to dump our refuse.

Take Action

You

— avoid products with excessive packaging
— always take a shopping bag to the shops with you, so avoiding consumption of extra plastic carriers
— buy products packaged in easily recyclable materials; glass or paper, not plastic
— when buying paper products opt for those made with recycled paper, ie toilet paper, stationery, tissues. Ensure that the newspapers you buy are printed on recycled paper
— write to manufacturers informing them of your choice and encouraging them to sell goods packaged in recyclable materials
— insist that your supermarket or local shops only stock goods in containers that can be returned or recycled

The Government

— the establishment of adequate collection sites for glass, paper, plastics and cans
— implementation of the EEC guidelines on the 'polluter pays' principle
— a ban on imported waste
— adequate waste control procedures to ensure safety regulations are not infringed.

Chapter 8

Endangered Species

Survival of the fittest is the law of the jungle and one by which all animals, including humans, are bound. If animals can't adapt to change then they will die out just as the dinosaurs did. Over the centuries a number of species have become extinct, among them the Mexican grizzly bear, great auk and passenger pigeon.

But now the animal world is facing its biggest ever challenge — to stay alive in a world dominated by greedy and thoughtless humans armed with guns, explosives, machines and money. Will the world's 4,589 species currently under threat become as dead as dodos? The race for survival has begun.

The world supports an astonishing amount of life. Scientists have identified and studied 1.4 million animal species and estimate that there are between another ten and 30 million species in existence, many of these insects and invertebrates. Research in the Panamanian rainforest suggests that there could be another 30 million undiscovered insects, totally unique to the rainforests.

> *The worst wildlife depletion occured prior to the Second World War before conservation was even recognised. The whole concept of conserving resources for the future has developed since then and now people are considering the ethical aspect of our relationship with animals.*
> Martin Harvey, International Whaling Commission

Half of all animal extinctions have occurred this century and it is believed that another one million species could be lost by the year 2000, which works out at over 270 extinctions every day for the next ten years. The world has seen off ten mammals in the last ten years including the Falkland Island wolf, the Syrian wild ass and the crescent nail-tail wallaby.

The situation is extremely serious. In 1988 the IUCN (International Union for Conservation of Nature and Natural Resources) updated its Red List of endangered animals. The numbers are staggering — 555 mammals, 1073 birds, 186 reptiles, 54 amphibians, 596 fishes and 2125 invertebrates.

According to the IUCN monitoring data, animals on the brink of extinction are the black rhino of Africa, a wild Asian ox known as the kouprey, the greater bamboo lemur from Madagascar, the South American highland guan — a member of the pheasant family — the Philippines eagle, the salmon crested cockatoo from Indonesia and the southeast Asian river terrapin. These animals are just a handful from the diversity of the natural world and have been hounded to near extinction by trade, disappearing habitat and hunting.

The loss of habitat worldwide has undoubtedly had a tragic effect on many animals. Human beings have encroached on almost every part of the world. Environmentalists are campaigning for Antarctica to be awarded World Park status before exploration companies wreak havoc on the huge colonies of wildlife. The rapid loss of the rainforests (11-15 million hectares every year) is incalculable, as a habitat they contain almost half of all known animal species.

For example the Philippines eagle is totally dependent on the rainforests, it nests in ferns growing on tall trees and feeds on flying lemurs, large snakes, hornbills, civets and monkeys. The greater bamboo lemur lives in the Madagascan rainforest and has been affected by the decline in giant bamboo stems which are now used up by human settlements.

Seas around the world are polluted with toxic wastes and are overfished. The beautiful coral reefs are being destroyed by local people selling mementoes to tourists. Building, agriculture and dams have also taken their toll. The African national parks are shrinking and animals can no longer roam as they once did; and poachers run riot. Species that developed within a narrow environment such as the Galapagos Islands are being squeezed out.

The wildlife kingdom has paid a high price for supplying man with food and products; classic examples of this are whaling, the ivory trade, fur coats, tortoise shell and reptile skins used for handbags and shoes. Many species of bird were virtually wiped out in the early part of the century to supply the demand for decorative feathers. The trade in wild animals as pets and status symbols has increased dramatically over the last century to the point at which many animals are now very rare and in danger of being wiped out.

An endangered female black rhinoceros and calf, Ngorongoro Crater, Tanzania. (*World Wide Fund for Nature*).

All 36 species of big cat are either vulnerable or endangered and the tiger, the cheetah, the snow leopard, the jaguar and the cougar are now facing extinction. Rhino numbers have declined by 90 per cent since the 1970s as a result of being hunted for their horn. Of the five rhino species there are just over 8,000 left, Javan rhinos number 50 and Sumatran rhinos 800.

Trade in animals

The USA, Japan and the European Community are the main markets in which these animals and their products are sold. The Western World has the economic control over demand and should therefore take responsibility for endangered species. Developing countries are often very poor in comparison, with little foreign currency, and supplying indigenous wildlife to relatively rich Westerners is worth millions of pounds every year.

The legislation that exists to protect endangered species is often inadequate and lacks proper enforcement. At the moment trade in wild animals and plants is mainly controlled by the CITES treaty (the Convention on International Trade in Endangered Species of Wild Fauna and Flora). CITES was set up in 1975 and now has 102 signatories including the European member states and the USA. The treaty classifies heavily traded animals into three categories:

— Appendix 1 for animals threatened with extinction
— Appendix 2 for those considered vulnerable
— Appendix 3 when a species is protected by its home country. Theoretically no other country can allow the listed animal in without an export permit.

Trade in Appendix 1 animals is completely forbidden, this group includes the great apes, rhinos, Asian elephants, sea turtles, the great whales, the giant panda, the big cats, some lizards, crocodiles, monkeys and birds of prey. Animals in Appendix 2 include monkeys, cats, otters, dolphins, porpoises, killer whales, tortoises, parrots and the African elephant which are subject to export licences and quotas.

In the UK the CITES Management Authority is the Department of the Environment; it issues permits and writes annual reports on wildlife trade. But it is left up to the Customs and Excise to implement on-site inspection and seizure of animals. However each country has different laws and regulations and some are more lax than others. Often customs do not have sufficient manpower to carry out a proper inspection.

The illegal trade is estimated to account for one third of the world's buoyant market for wildlife. Export and import licences are forged, people paid off and endangered species or their products smuggled in. If traders are arrested for breaking regulations and taken to court it's highly unlikely they will be sent to prison and fines are usually very low. The deterrents against traders importing and exporting are minimal.

Added to the difficulty of implementing blanket controls are the following factors: few ports of entry have any animal holding facilities, making it impossible for animals to be kept back; customs staff often do not have the necessary background to identify an endangered animal; and containers can be difficult to examine and endangered species can be smuggled in with other animals.

Cruel practices

The Environmental Investigation Agency (EIA), a British conservation group, has made a close study of the wildlife trade and has revealed some horrific transport practices. The CITES regulations state that 'Management Authorities of the Parties shall be satisfied that any living specimen will be so prepared and shipped as to minimise the risk of injury, damage to health or cruel treatment'. Often this is not the case and many animals die during long journeys or afterwards in quarantine.

Birds which are sold into the pet trade are notoriously badly treated. The EIA has collected evidence from Senegal, the world's largest bird exporting country, which shows that half the birds caught die before they have even reached the airport for export. This is due to injury, overcrowding, lack of food and water and the shock of being caged.

Once prepared for export, consignments of birds are often packed into sub-standard crates for days on end without adequate food and water. Birds become dehydrated very quickly and their water supplies soon run out, they are crammed together so tightly that their body heat is suffocating and the unlucky ones die. Death during transport and in quarantine account for a further 20 per cent of each batch. For the ones that manage to survive very few live longer than a year and so the bird trade is perpetuated by owners buying a replacement bird.

An endangered species of bird,
the Moluccan Cockatoo.

Some exported birds are endangered and as such are worth thousands of pounds to collectors. Included are the large parrots such as the hyacinth macaw, canidi macaw and palm cockatoo and 87 of the 287 species of birds of prey. Out of 329 parrot species, 30 face extinction. Birds can often be diseased on arrival and pass on infections to humans such as psitticosis, tuberculosis and hepatitis.

The IATA (International Air Transport Association) does not help matters as members consistently break the CITES regulations and the IATA's own Live Animals Regulations. Consignments that are shipped according to the rule books are the exception rather than the rule.

Traders get away with such cruel treatment because of the general lack of control and concern on the part of airlines and airports. Heathrow, which has implemented some controls, is avoided by traders who realise that a stop over could result in a costly hold up and even prosecution. But even Heathrow has a long way to go.

In 1985 the EIA published *Injury, Damage to Health and Cruel Treatment*, a report on the appalling conditions of transported wildlife. On the international scene nothing much has changed over the past five years, here are some examples of what they found:

1. Ten giant squirrels were imported from Indonesia by a British zoo, the animals were stuffed into narrow plastic tubes no bigger than their bodies and stacked in a wooden crate. Two squirrels died in transit, the rest were in poor condition on arrival.
2. Two crates containing 1,000 Garter snakes were shipped from Miami to London. One crate contained 800 snakes; on arrival only two were alive. Out of the remaining 200 packed into the second crate only 76 survived. The dead snakes were crushed and suffocated by the sheer weight of their fellows. The pitiful 78 survivors died within days of arrival.
3. Ten Canadian river otters were shipped from Canada to the UK, due to unsuitable crates only two survived.
4. Twenty flamingoes were shipped from Tanzania to London, on arrival three were dead, the other 17 had suffered multiple wounds to legs and wings from tight, non-elastic straps.
5. A shipment of 2,000 lovebirds was sent to London from Tanzania, packed 80-90 to a crate, 400 birds were dead on arrival.
6. Twenty-nine squirrel monkeys arrived in Japan from Bolivia. Fifteen of the monkeys had tied their tails into a giant knot and had to be anaesthetised while a vet took 20 minutes to undo it. Three monkeys at the bottom of the huddle were dead and three more died soon after arrival.

The African elephant, primates and whales and dolphins are some of our favourite animal species, yet even these are vulnerable to extinction. They all have been, and are being, exploited by humans and may join the ranks of the extinct if steps are not taken to protect them.

The African Elephant

In 1979 there were 1.5 million elephants living in Africa, now there are only 600,000. They have suffered wholesale slaughter for the sake of the ivory trade. In 1988/89 only 20 per cent of ivory traded was legal and two thirds of that was snatched from poachers. The remaining 78 per cent was poached and laundered into the system.

Elephants have been wiped out from Western and Northern Africa and are acutely endangered in Eastern Africa. Countries such as Tanzania, Kenya, Zaire and Uganda have been badly hit, and governments have not helped by confiscating ivory and then selling it back into the market. There has been widespread corruption in the ivory trade.

African elephant population

Last century	10,000,000
1970	2,000,000
1979	1,300,000
1989	650,000

Value of ivory

1969	$ 5.45 per kilo
1970	$ 7.44
1978	$ 75.00
1989	$200.00

Source: Elefriends

If a young elephant under the age of nine loses its mother it will probably die, very few orphans survive. And it has been estimated that in Tanzania one elephant family in three are orphans. Once the poachers have killed off the big male tuskers, they turn to the younger males for ivory. But male elephants only mature at around 30 years old and their many deaths have disrupted patterns of reproduction. The average tusk weight has dropped from 20kg to just 4.5kg in the past 20 years.

Poachers ambush elephants, machine-gun them and then hack their tusks out. They have been known to kill mothers in the throes of giving birth, and park rangers run the risk of losing their own lives if set upon by poachers. And as the elephant population falls, so the price of ivory rises. Illegally poached ivory is smuggled out of Africa via the United Arab Emirates and, up until mid-1989, was sold on to Japan, Hong Kong, Taiwan, Korea and Singapore where it was made into trinkets, carvings and piano keys.

1989 saw a sustained effort by campaigners and some African governments to stop the slaughter of elephants for their tusks. An ivory ban was supported by the EEC, the USA, Japan and Hong Kong midway through 1989 and now the African elephant has been placed on the CITES Appendix 1 list. There will be a two-year moratorium on the ivory trade and Japan, the biggest retail outlet of ivory, is supporting the ban. The situation will be reviewed again at the next CITES meeting in 1992. However, the ban does not cover the hunting and culling of elephants.

Primates

There are 200 species of primate, 90 per cent of them living in the tropical rainforests of Asia, Africa and South and Central America. Man is a primate and is at the top of the range of species, followed by gorillas, orang-utans and chimpanzees; tarsiers and lemurs represent the lower end of development. The World Wide Fund for Nature has estimated that 14 per cent of the known 200 species are highly endangered and could be extinct by the year 2000 and that 34 per cent are becoming increasingly vulnerable.

The eleven regional communities of African primates

Source: IUCN

The biggest threat is from loss of habitat because the rainforests are being chopped down at such a fast rate. Mountain gorillas are on the verge of extinction, along with the golden lion tamarin, the muriqui, the indri and the aye-aye. Sadly, one of the most prized wildlife trophies remains the head of a mountain gorilla.

Humans hunting for food, medicine, skins and ornamentation have placed many primates under considerable threat in the Amazon region, Western and Central Africa. In Amazonia woolly monkeys and spider monkeys have been wiped out by over-hunting. Medical research has also put pressure on chimpanzee and cotton-top tamarin populations, many are captured live and exported for experimentation because biologically they are so similar to humans.

It is believed that chimpanzee colonies in Western Africa have been put under severe strain by live export trade for medical research. The chimp is very important to medical research because it has the same blood groups as humans, and a large brain to bodyweight ratio. In order to catch a few babies, trappers will frequently kill whole families and the orphan chimps often die in transit. Many campaigners feel that chimps for scientific purposes should be bred in captivity, to avoid draining the wild resources.

Whales, Dolphins and Porpoises

This group is known as the cetaceans and comprises 77 different species, ranging from the common dolphin to the blue whale. The cetaceans are divided into two groups: the baleen whales which have whalebone instead of teeth and the toothed whales. There are 11 varieties of baleen whale and all the great whales are included in this category; the blue, the right, the grey, the bowhead, the sei, the fin, the humpback, and the minke.

The remaining 66 are toothed whales and are also termed small cetaceans (except the sperm whale, which although it has teeth is classified as a great whale). This range includes all dolphins, porpoises, narwhals, pilot and killer whales.

The great whales

1 Sperm Whale
2 Grey Whale
3 Minke Whale
4 Brydes Whale
5 Sei Whale
6 Fin Whale
7 Blue Whale
8 Humpback Whale
9 Black Right Whale
10 Bowhead Whale

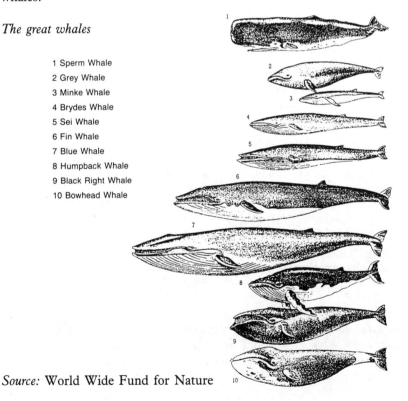

Source: World Wide Fund for Nature

Whaling has been practiced since the ninth century and reached a peak in the 1960s. Worldwide, over a million great whales have been killed this century for their oil and meat. Over 300,000 blue whales were killed in the first half of the century and despite 30 years of protection have not yet recovered. Present day numbers are believed to be between 200 and 1,100. The bowhead whale has been reduced to five per cent of its original population even though it lives in distant Arctic seas. And the right whale has been so heavily hunted that its numbers have been reduced to three per cent of original stock.

The fate of the great whales has not been a happy one and in the 1970s scientists and conservationists began to express deep concern over their dwindling numbers. In 1986 the International Whaling Commission, which has responsibility for the baleen whales, declared a moratorium on commercial whaling of the 11 great whales so that stock could be assessed. Supporters of the regulation, which included the UK, claimed that alternatives existed for every whale product.

The moratorium lasts until 1990 and it is quite likely to continue after that date, although minke whales may be hunted again. However Japan and Iceland have taken advantage of a loophole in the regulation which says that a certain number of whales can be killed for scientific purposes. Several hundred whales have been harpooned under this guise since the moratorium.

Although the great whales may be relatively safe for a while the International Whaling Commission regulation does not cover any of the small cetaceans which are being slaughtered in huge numbers around the world. The Whale and Dolphin Conservation Society estimate that hundreds of thousands of porpoises, dolphins and other small cetaceans are killed each year.

Nearly 20,000 small cetaceans are killed annually just for sport and in the tuna industry in the Eastern Pacific around 130,000 dolphins are killed each year, the helpless victims of fish nets. The tuna fish swim beneath schools of dolphins, fishermen do not discriminate and scoop up the whole lot in their nets. Many small cetaceans are also caught up in 'ghost' nets, fishing nets that have drifted loose and floated out to sea.

Much closer to home, sightings of dolphins and porpoises around British coastal waters are rapidly decreasing, although 12 species are regularly seen. Cardigan Bay, once famed for its dolphins, is now polluted with raw sewage and animal wastes. In 1988 a baby dolphin was found floating in the Bay, it had died from toxic hepatitis and its body was heavily contaminated with organochlorines. Bottlenosed dolphins living around the Dornoch Firth in West Scotland are threatened by encroaching pollution from a sewage outfall pipe near Chanonry Point where dolphins congregate.

People are now waking up to the fact that the natural world is our primary source and has got to be conserved if man is to continue. It is vital to our own health and welfare. Development can continue, but alongside conservation, so that those who depend on natural resources can continue to do so.
Sally Nicholson, World Wide Fund For Nature

Humans are at the top of the food chain and because of that occupy a very special and responsible position. We are capable of rational thought and of bringing change. The wildlife that we so carelessly destroy has as much right to be on the planet as us and should be respected — we still have much to learn about them. It's time to act on a global basis; we, the Western consumers, must cut the demand for wild and endangered species as pets and products. Without prompt action, the zoo may be the only place where a safari is possible.

Take Action
You
— don't fuel the pet trade in exotic animals. Birds, snakes, lizards, fish and monkeys are wild animals which adapt badly to a caged life. Birds and monkeys also carry disease. For each live animal you see in the pet shop many others may have died as a result of capture
— as far as possible avoid buying animal products such as coral, ivory, tortoiseshell, reptile skin shoes and handbags, fur coats and any fancy goods which contain any of these. You are only encouraging the trade in animal exploitation, some of which are endangered and many vulnerable
— avoid any whale products and tuna fish. Whale hunting is unnecessary and tuna fishing wipes out over a hundred thousand dolphins every year
The Government
— call for greater enforcement of the CITES treaty around the world. Also insist on airlines sticking to the IATA Live Animals Regulations
— provide better facilities for examining and ensuring humane methods of transport for imported animals
— join with other countries in supporting developing countries against poaching and trade in endangered species
— ban the sale of exotic animals in pet shops
— clean up Britain's coastal waters
— support a continued moratorium on hunting the great whales, and push for a similar body to the International Whaling Commission to take responsibility for the 66 small cetaceans currently unprotected
— review the import of live monkeys, particularly chimpanzees, for medical research.

Chapter 9

Disappearing Countryside

The British Isles have been conquered by all manner of people from the Vikings, to the Picts, the Celts, the Saxons, the Romans and the Normans. The Spanish, the French and lastly the Germans have also eyed our lands with a warlike gaze. Why does this small island arouse such interest?

Could it be that the natural wealth visible throughout the land is just too much to ignore? The green pastures, the shimmering lakes, the dales and valleys, the towering mountains and the miles and miles of coastline. Fertile, varied and highly desirable? It's a good enough reason. Britain has an envious diversity of natural landscapes. Ireland, Scotland, Wales and England all proudly sport their own individual beauty.

But like the tale of the three little pigs, a wolf stands snarling at the door. All is not apple pie and cherry ripe. For rural Britain faces the massed ranks of developers, poised for action with diggers and cranes. Leisure complexes, holiday homes, new towns, barn conversions, roads, open cast mining, the Channel Tunnel link and fish farms... the face of Britain's countryside is changing, and could be trampled to unrecognition if the developers have their way.

Since the end of World War II change has run amok, and the inventory of countryside loss is phenomenal. England alone has lost 95 per cent of lowland grassland, 50 per cent of lowland fens, 40 per cent of broadleaved woodland, 109,000 miles of hedgerow in England and Wales, and 5,000 miles of stone walls. An area the size of Berkshire, Buckinghamshire, Oxfordshire and Bedfordshire has been put in a concrete overcoat.

For the past 43 years, since the Town and Country Planning Act of 1947, agriculture and forestry have been exempt from most of the Act's planning controls. As a result, farmers and foresters, custodians of the countryside, have got away with rather a lot. Barns, silos, milking parlours, roads and slurry tanks are just some of the farm additions that don't need planning permission. Hedges have been pulled out, stone walls pulled down, all for the sake of productivity and with not a whimper of opposition from successive governments.

In the 1990s, the uncontrolled use of land could expand even further. Due to agricultural surpluses, the concept of Set Aside (taking land out of production) has been introduced throughout the EEC. Instead of allowing a less intensive programme of farming to evolve or encouraging wildlife habitats, many farmers are using Set Aside land for urban style development — for residential, industrial and transport purposes. Between 1977 and 1986, the Ministry of Agriculture (MAFF) opposed most applications for large-scale development on the best UK farmland but, by 1987, a sudden swing in the opposite direction saw MAFF allowing five times more applications than it opposed.

According to its remit from the 1986 Agriculture Act, MAFF is supposed to balance the needs of conservation with agriculture, which it is blatantly not doing. Even in relation to poorer types of land, MAFF agreed to 100 times more applications for development than it objected to. Traditionally MAFF has stood guard over the richest and the poorest land to retain its agricultural potential. In the future, the time may come when we need that land back again for growing food, but if the top-soil has been damaged by development it will be worse than useless.

It is quite obvious that planning control over agriculture is not strong enough. And rather than iron out the problems, the Government is intending to add to them if the latest secondary legislation Consultation Paper — Permitted Use Rights In The Countryside — is anything to go by. In its present form (it will hopefully be amended), the paper suggests even more farmland diversification that will not be subject to planning controls.

The type of new installations that will be allowed if the paper becomes law are farm shops, sport and recreation facilities for activities such as clay pigeon shooting, BMX bikes and wargames, car parks, refreshment areas and educational centres would also burgeon. Rather than constructing new buildings which would be subject to planning control, existing buildings can be converted and the use of the land simply changed. If this goes ahead it could herald the coming of even larger developments, such as theme parks, zoos and safari parks, where permanent buildings do not have to be erected.

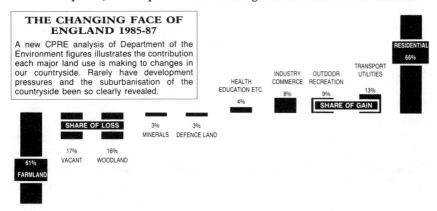

Source: The Council for the Protection of Rural England.

The Council for the Protection of Rural England (CPRE) acts as the nation's independent guard dog on such matters and has major doubts as to the benefit of these proposals should they become law. Far from saying that these types of facility have no place in the countryside, the CPRE believes that sensitive planning is the key to stop development going out of control.

If there's money to be made though, developments will understandably blossom on every available acre of land, spoiling the countryside for all those who just want a little peace and quiet. The Countryside Commission, the government's advisory body, has similar feelings and in its report, *Planning for a Greener Countryside*, comments that 'problems often arise because the development is inappropriate for the proposed site ... imposed on the countryside rather than being a part of it'.

Barn conversions are another area of dubious benefit. A study commissioned by the CPRE called *Superb Conversions?* concluded that the five arguments used to justify the conversion of a farm building are often not met on completion of the renovation. These are:

★ the provision of employment
★ the supply of rural housing
★ farm income support
★ the preservation of traditional and historic buildings
★ the encouragement of farm diversification and new land uses

The study found that the impact of conversion on local employment is minimal, particularly if it is done by the farmer's family rather than a local company. The argument that converted barns provide housing for rural communities is well and truly scotched by the average price of conversions — well beyond the means of local people. As for the farmer's own income increasing, it was found that larger farmers reap better financial benefits from converting more buildings, compared to smaller farmers who just received a one-off cash injection.

Strangely, few barns had been converted into craft or light industry centres, the rent on which would provide a permanent income for the farmer. Keeping the building's historic aspect was not always achieved and as most of the barns were converted for residential purposes it was necessary to pay careful attention to planning and design to retain the original character, and this was not always done.

March of the conifers

Since 1919, great armies of faceless conifers have stamped their way across the highlands and the lowlands, Sitka spruce now covers half a million hectares and makes up 52 per cent of conifers planted by the Forestry Commission in Scotland and Wales. In Scotland, according to 1987 figures from the Forestry Commission, 918,000 hectares of land are covered in conifers compared to 78,000 hectares of traditional broadleaved trees. In Wales, there are almost three times as many conifers than broadleaves.

Afforestation began between the two World Wars to provide Britain with home-grown wood, particularly for pit props; used in the trenches. That purpose rapidly became defunct, but the afforestation continued with thousands of acres being planted since that time, at the expense of many of our ancient broadleaved woodlands that nurture diversity.

However, it is fair to say that the Forestry Commission has become more sympathetic to the needs of the land and is now encouraging the planting of more broadleaved trees. No more coniferous planting is occurring in northern England, but is still going on in Scotland and Wales. Tax relief on forest ownership has also been abolished due to the media uproar of 1988 when it was revealed that celebrities and business corporations were investing in conifer plantations as a tax dodge.

National Parks

Recipients of many conifers have been the National Parks which now find themselves under serious threat from developers instead of trees. There are 11 National Parks, covering a tenth of England and Wales, they are:

★ the Lake District
★ the Peak District
★ the North York Moors
★ Dartmoor
★ Exmoor
★ the Yorkshire Dales

★ Snowdonia
★ Pembrokeshire
★ the Breacon Beacons
★ Northumberland
★ the Norfolk Broads

The idea of a National Park is to preserve its natural assets such as moorland, lakes, and woods for the public to enjoy. The tourist boards see these areas as economic resources where development brings money. And here lies a fundamental difference of opinion — how should a National Park operate? It's true to say that tourism brings jobs and a strong local economy, but the tourism of today is conducted on a grand scale, unknown in the past.

It has never been the policy of National Parks to accept large housing estates, but applications for tourist complexes are now cropping up with alarming frequency at planning meetings. At the moment the Parks have to prove that a proposed development is not in keeping with the environment if they want to turn down planning applications. The Council for National Parks would like to see a situation similar to that in America, where the onus is on the developer to prove that his proposal is in the interest of the park, that it is necessary and also appropriate.

> *The Parks come first. Wherever competing interests conflict, the Parks are the priority. the National Parks are not ours, but ours to look after, ours to treasure and enjoy.*
> Brian Redhead, President of the Council for National Parks

The Council believes that the Government does not give sufficient back-up to the Parks authorities and should place an outright ban on certain types of development without further ado. Because of the clash between the interests of tourist boards and Parks, there is a clear argument that tourism in these areas should be controlled by the Parks authorities alone.

Multiplying timeshare complexes are the biggest development to assault a number of National Parks. The Lake District in particular has been pinpointed as an area ripe for the picking. In 1981 the first large timeshare complex opened at Langdale, helped by a tourist board grant. It covers 35 acres and includes 82 self-catering 'Norwegian' style lodges and the Langdale Hotel. The *pièce de résistance* is an all-weather leisure oasis, palm fringed with a Caribbean atmosphere.

This is what the Council for National Parks thought of Langdale: 'Langdale is not an eyesore. It is a "quality" development. It is "the most sought-after timeshare in Europe". It won a Civic Trust award in 1986. It could even be represented as an environmental improvement of a run down site. But it offers a pastiche of international leisure cultures — the Caribbean beach, the Norwegian chalet. It represents a scale of commercial activity which threatens the quiet sanctuary of the National Parks.'

The pill for such development is often sweetened with promises for the local people. When Langdale was a planner's dream, locals were to have use of the facilities. What did that mean in 1989? It meant that locals could take out an annual seven-day family membership for just £480 — a mere snip, and that the town school could use the pool once a week, free.

The development at Keswick Bridge (Swedish style lodges, a tropical pool and various eateries) was hailed as a marvellous opportunity for the community, who were wooed with the promise of a brand new swimming pool. The project has since floundered leaving the local ratepayers with a bill of £6 million and a measly 'splash' pool in which to drown their sorrows. The land had originally been set aside for housing.

Recent surveys in the Lake District have shown that the majority of visitors do not come for these 'tourist attractions' but rather for the fresh air and breathtaking scenery. They do not want commercialisation, if anything it is this that will drive them away. The Lake District has two other big complexes (over 60 lodges) — Windermere Marina and the Lakeland Village, Backbarrow.

The Friends of the Lake District feel that these developments are 'obstructive in the landscape' and have been incensed by the Marina which is right on the Bowness shore of Lake Windermere. Members question the logic of enticing even more tourists into an area which already has 12 million people passing through every year. And the problem reaches even further into the local community when developers start to snap up adjacent buildings, with the direct result that local people can no longer afford to live there.

The Pembrokeshire Coast, Exmoor, and the North York Moors have the added problem of a flourishing fish farming industry. As with other types of agriculture, fish farming does not come under the normal planning controls. The ludicrous situation currently exists that, if a National Park does reject a fish farm application, it has to pay compensation to the farmer. A costly and illogical drain on its scant resources.

Both marine and freshwater varieties of fish are farmed. The armoury of chemicals that are put into the tanks, fungicides especially, and the effluent from fish can cause local pollution. A ten-fold increase in fish farming is expected in Milford Haven, Pembrokeshire, over the next couple of years and, already, sizeable plots of land have been given over to the business. Fish farms create a further blot on the landscape by using floodlighting and unsightly cages, not to mention the often elaborate defence systems to ward off poachers.

Country dwellers

But fish are not the only animals migrating to the countryside. Human beings are arriving in their droves and last year saw considerable debate over the ethics of building new towns in the countryside to accommodate the overflow. Research has shown that 80 per cent of the population would prefer to live in the country rather than in a city or urban town.

The Department of the Environment has calculated that, by the year 2001, two million extra houses will have to be built, 570,000 of those in the south-east, which has had to fit in half the population growth of England and Wales. Every county council has to provide what is termed a Structure Plan for the next 10 years. This plan identifies exactly where the council is planning developments and has to show existing free land available for the next five years.

Land under threat. Housing estates at edge of Canford Heath, near Bournemouth. Developments continue to encroach the British heathlands.

The CPRE believes that enough land has already been provided for in the Structure Plans of the south east to meet these requirements and that there is in fact a 38 per cent over-supply of land. One of the reasons behind this seemingly illogical situation in such an over-populated area is that councils are not legally allowed to take into account small sites (aptly termed 'wind-fall' sites) that may have become derelict or vacant which actually provide a large amount of free land. Councils can also infill existing built-up areas and revitalise inner urban areas. This means that more land than needed is planned for.

The south east of England has come under exceptional pressure from new housing proposals. One of the most widely publicised cases was that of Stone Bassett in Oxfordshire. The proposals for the luckless Stone Bassett infuriated the surrounding villagers and tested the strength of UK planning controls to the limit.

Oversupply of housing land in south east region (windfall sites)	
1983	8% oversupply
1984	17% oversupply
1985	23% oversupply
1986	29% oversupply
1987	32% oversupply
1988	30% oversupply
Source: SERPLAN	

Consortium Developments Ltd, a company established by Bovis, Barratt, Wimpey and Beazer, was behind the spectre of Stone Bassett and fought long and hard for permission to develop an area of 12,000 acres and build 6,000 houses. Within the package were a country park, leisure centre, swimming pool, schools and health care — all thrown in. But Stone Bassett bit the dust, the case against the development was taken up by some of the highest paid planners in the land and sounded a massive victory for conservationists.

The same happened to Foxley Wood (Hampshire) and Tillingham Hall (Essex), new towns that would have been a dream come true for some people, but which were deemed unjustifiable and unnecessary by the Government inspector of planning appeals. The developers tend to argue that country living offers people a good quality of life, and that they are relieving pressure on towns which are bursting at the seams, such as Reading, Camberley and Swindon. This may be so but, once one developer has been let in, the decision could open the floodgate for scores of unsuitable, unnecessary applications.

> *It is the government's policy to reduce the burden of controls on businesses and individuals whenever possible. This is a theme of our approach to planning. An equally important aim is to ensure that the planning system continues to protect and enhance the environment.*
> Christopher Chope, Environment Minister (May 1989)

A new town may physically take up a small space, but the end result can be seen from far and wide. These new towns proposed all over the country have been called 'a solution in search of a problem' by the CPRE — in other words a solution to a non-existent problem, as enough land has already been put aside for people to be housed. But the Government likes to submit to free market forces and developers attempt to respond, rather than taking into account where new homes should be built in the best interests of the public.

However there are cases where new towns may be the best option. For example a potential 3,000 house settlement between Cambridge and Ely offers the best means to provide more housing. New towns are not just being proposed in the properous south-east either. To the west of York a 3,000 house development has been mooted for Acaster Malbis, a disused airfield. Between Wetherby and Thorp Arch, a 7,000 house settlement may be built.

It's possible to draw a comparison between York and the National Parks: some countryside campaigners feel that the city has over-promoted itself in terms of business opportunities and pleasant surroundings. If it develops too fast York may kill the goose that laid the golden egg and no one will want to live there — just as tourists are beginning to avoid Lake Windermere because of its commerciality and crowds of people.

There is also increasing pressure on the country's greenbelt areas. Fifteen greenbelts in England and five in Scotland cover 4.5 million acres of often prime land. The greenbelts have so far ensured that towns and cities do not sprawl into one another. Only a few miles out of London there are green fields and woods, due to strong observation of greenbelt principles by the Government and councils.

The Great Glade, Hayley Wood, Cambridgeshire, an ancient woodland. The vegetation layers — canopy, shrub and field — are clearly visible.

But greenbelts are gradually being encroached upon. In the south-east, redundant hospitals are becoming vacant and the developers are moving in.

In Shenley, Hertfordshire, and Epsom, Surrey, plans are afoot to build residential houses, even though the plots of land are right smack inside the greenbelt. Chester, in particular, is making loud noises about converting some of its greenbelt for housing and light industry. York has similar ideas.

Rambling roads

Roads are a vitally important aspect of the UK's infrastructure, but have become an obsession with some people. The latest White Paper to come from the Ministry of Transport is called *Roads for Prosperity*. A more appropriate title would be *Roads to Nowhere*. In an effort to ease congestion, the Government is spending an estimated £12 billion on building 900 miles of new roads. It is also proposed that widescale improvements and expansions to existing roads should take place in the next decade.

If the White Paper becomes an Act of Parliament, the whole of the M5 and nearly all of the M1 will be widened to take four lanes in each direction. Other widening projects include the M62, the M42, the M11, the M4 and the M2. Environmentalists are agreed that more roads encourage more cars. It has been predicted that, by 2025, vehicles on the road will have increased by over 100 per cent. Do we really want all these cars and all these journeys, polluting the air we breathe, creating endless noise and accidents, as well as eating up energy? Why not spend some of that money on improving public transport schemes — more energy efficient, safer and less polluting?

Water Privatisation could well add to the list of threats against the countryside. The Water Authorities own over 430,000 acres of land, which, once in private hands, will be an extremely valuable asset. Land could be sold off or developed, causing significant harm to present areas of natural beauty and important wildlife habitats. One hopes that privatisation would not result in such measures being taken and that the independent monitoring body — the National Rivers Authority — will have enough bite to stop it from happening. But looking at the past track record of the present Government, one can't help wondering.

The EEC steps in

It is also hoped that the EEC may have some positive move to make towards more vigilant preservation of our countryside. The EEC Habitat Directive, although not yet in force, proposes an element of control over such things as hedgerows, dry stone walls and heathland. In 1987 the UK Government went back on a pre-election promise to introduce Landscape Conservation Orders to protect these areas, so proper control from the EEC would be most welcome. Meadows and woodlands are better looked after, but that still leaves many different habitats that do not have sufficient protection.

The Habitat Directive would seek to improve this situation, but sadly the UK is kicking up a fuss about the depth of the proposal, which simply wishes to preserve our natural heritage. Undoubtedly the 1981 Wildlife and Countryside Act has already had a beneficial effect on our countryside and wild animals, but it is not enough. However, the Countryside Commission, the Government's advisory body, is making strenuous efforts to impress upon everyone the need for sensitivity when dealing with development.

No-one is denying that development shouldn't go on, as change is inevitable. What environmentalists are saying is that change should not be made for the benefit of a few and to the detriment of many. Rather than fat cat developers benefiting from the countryside, small businesses and local people should have the main part to play in sensitive development.

In such a small country it is up to the Government to take a strong stand against unsuitable developments. The National Parks need backing, so do the greenbelts and the remaining countryside. These problems are in the nation's very own back yard; theme parks, tourist accommodation, recreation, housing all have their rightful place. But in the Lake District, in Snowdonia? Some things remain sacred don't they?

Take Action
You
— nice as they may sound, avoid buying timeshare flats in the National Parks
— write to your MP highlighting the problems excluding certain agricultural activities from planning controls
— request that farm shops, recreational facilities, and car parks should come under proper planning controls
— support the organic farming movement (see Chapter 10) to stop Set Aside farmland being over-developed and covered in concrete
— the only way to relieve congestion on the roads is to get off them. Think about cycling more, or travelling on public transport
The Government
— accept the EEC Habitat Directive
— categorically refuse any attempts to build unsuitable tourist developments in the National Parks
— transform the Ministry of 'roads' into a true Ministry of Transport
— further encourage the planting of native broadleaved woods
— closely monitor the new private water companies in their use of land
— closely regulate housing developments in the countryside.

Chapter 10

Farming and Agriculture

Over the last forty years, farming has developed into a highly intensive manufacturing business. The soil is pushed beyond its capabilities with nitrogen fertilisers, crops are sprayed with highly toxic chemicals to prevent damage from insects, disease and fungus, and from birth animals join an endless, often cruel production line that denies them any dignity. The West exports the philosophy of intensive farming to developing countries, resulting in chemical dependence, over-production and degradation of the land. In the EEC, food surpluses are commonplace, leading to disposal of thousands of tonnes of food every year.

It is becoming painfully clear, despite the millions pumped into research and development, that intensive farming does not provide the perfect solution to feeding mouths. In the light of recent scares about pesticide residues in food, nitrates in drinking water, and food poisoning in eggs, cheese and other foods, it seems that agricultural standards are due for an urgent review. A review on the part of government, farms and us, the consumers.

Chemicals

Take the soil. Chemical treatment with nitrogen, potassium and phosphate was introduced just before the war to increase production in a time when manpower was low. Use of these fertilisers has increased by eight times since the 1950s, and allows farmers to grow one crop continuously without letting the ground recuperate.

An average crop has between 100 and 400kg per hectare of nitrogen deposited on it every year, and between 70 and 150kg per hectare is leached into the ground and filters through to the water systems. Nitrogen can take up to 20 years to pollute water and, therefore, is a very long term problem.

Water supplies to more than 1.7 million consumers currently exceed the EEC maximum level for nitrate (50mg per litre), and the Water Authorities Association has estimated that 9 per cent of farm land in East Anglia and the Midlands will be penalised by proposed EEC legislation to stop the rise of nitrates in deep ground waters. In relation to river pollution, the legislation will affect 80 per cent of the farm land in East Anglia and the Thames and

Severn Trent regions. It has been estimated that the average person in Europe and North America obtains 70 per cent of daily nitrate intake from vegetables and 21 per cent from drinking water. Lettuce and spinach are particularly vulnerable to nitrogen uptake.

Although arguments continue to rage over the effects of nitrogen on health, once digested through food or water it is suspected of having links with blue baby syndrome by reducing the oxygene-carrying capacity of the blood, and cancers of the stomach and oesophagus. Nitrate reacts with chemicals called amines which are present in our food to produce nitrosamines. These have a carcinogenic effect in 39 animal species, including primates. However, investigation into the effects on humans has, as yet, proved to be inconclusive.

The practice of pushing the soil beyond its capabilities combines with the aim of supplying blemish-free produce to create an industry dependent on pesticides, insecticides, fungicides and herbicides. There are over 1,000 compounds that a farmer can use on the land. And some of these have been linked with allergies and cancer. A controversy arose in early 1989 over the treatment of apples with the chemical Alar which was proved in animal tests to be carcinogenic. It has now been removed from sale by its makers, Uniroyal.

At the present time, the US Environmental Protection Agency is reassessing the safety of three widely used fungicides — maneb, mancozeb and zineb — again with suspicions of carcinogenic effects. These three fungicides are already on a UK Ministry of Agriculture (MAFF) list of 100 pesticides up for review, that have not been subject to modern tests. MAFF has promised a review of maneb, mancozeb and zineb after the Americans publish their report, but environmentalists argue that use of the chemicals should be suspended now.

Symptoms of pesticide poisoning in plants

Chemical	Symptoms
Amintriazole	Symptoms take up to 2 weeks to appear. Plants wilt, leaves pale then turn white (sometimes pinkish) starting at growing points and working down the leaf.
Clormequat	Stunting and sometimes almost complete suppression of growth occurs.
Contact herbicides	Scorching, yellowing and death of soft tissues occurs, especially at growing points, flowers, young leaves and fruitlets.
Glyphosphate	Symptoms slowly develop over 3-6 weeks. Stops growth, growing points yellow, wilting occurs, and die-back goes gradually down the plant.
'Hormone growth regulators'	Complete disruption of the growth process in many plants. Can also reduce the storage life of plants.
Paraquat/diquat	Circular, chlorotic spotting on leaves, followed by paling/yellowing. Some broad-leaved species quickly wilt, suffer interveinal discolouration and leaf edge blackening, browning and top-growth death.

Source: 'Drifting into Trouble' The Soil Association

MAFF's 1988 report on pesticide residues stated that residues were far higher than originally thought, particularly in the case of fruit and vegetables treated for storage. A research study from Cyprus showed that potatoes treated with a certain insecticide still contained a residue of 10 per cent (0.55mg per kg) in the skin after 16 weeks of storage. The World Health Organisation limit is 0.05mg per kg. Ninety-nine per cent of the pesticide was found in the skin. So all those of us who have been taught it is healthy to eat potato skins had better think again.

Toxic spray drift is another result of treating crops with pesticides. Miniscule droplets of the chemicals used can either drift during application, or evaporate after application and then drift onto neighbouring plants; alternatively granules and dust can be blown by strong gusts of wind onto other areas and into waterways. Spray drift can seriously damage neighbouring crops, livestock, wildlife and humans.

Many beehives have been destroyed by spray drift landing on the flowers from which bees collect pollen; timber treated with the household chemicals lindane and dieldrin (now banned from use) is extremely toxic to bats and continues to be so for decades after treatment, and many bat colonies have been eliminated in this way. Humans can be affected by pesticides through breathing in spray, brushing against treated plants and eating contaminated food. Symptoms include coughing, blurred vision, nausea, fits, faintness and skin rashes. The Nature Conservancy Council reports that 10 per cent of its Sites of Special Scientific Interest are annually contaminated by spray drift.

In addition to spray drift, intensive farming has a destructive effect on the surrounding fauna and flora. One fifth of British hedgerows and three quarters of wetland habitats have been lost so far. Soil structure has declined so much that in 1984 The Soil Survey of England and Wales calculated that 44 per cent of UK arable land was vulnerable to erosion. Rates of erosion up to 30 tonnes per hectare were recorded in some areas. Meadows rich in herbs can support up to 24 different species of butterfly, chemically treated fields can support none at all. Pesticides kill off the beneficial insects as well as the destructive ones creating an imbalance in nature and wasting valuable assets.

Common Agricultural Policy

Over the last decade, surpluses created by the EEC Common Agricultural Policy (CAP) have been a huge problem. The EEC spends 70 per cent of its budget on providing the funds to produce far more food than we need. There are frequent butter, grain, wine and beef mountains which are stored at great cost or sold off cheaply to other countries. Produce likely to go off, such as some fruits and vegetables, are destroyed.

The CAP was originally devised to protect the small, rural European farmer against larger and more efficient competitors. To achieve this aim, the CAP always guarantees a price for certain types of produce, so that, even if the produce sells at a poor price or is not sold at all, the farmer receives the going rate. On that basis, the CAP has not protected the small farmer because large, efficient farms have cashed in on the guaranteed payment scheme and produced huge quantities of food, using increasingly intensive methods. Added to this, a continual downward pressure on prices forces farmers to provide even more for even less.

In an attempt to reduce surpluses, the CAP has now introduced several new schemes for farmers. The Set Aside scheme for cereals, where farmers are paid to leave land fallow, and the extensification programme in which beef, sheep and wine farmers are paid to reduce output. Milk quotas imposed on dairy farmers have now stabilised, but only after putting many farmers out of business. There is grass roots doubt as to whether the Set Aside scheme can work, as the payment levels offered by the Ministry of Agriculture (MAFF) are not high enough. In the West German region of Lower Saxony, at payment levels £200 higher, only four per cent of eligible land has been taken out of production.

Livestock

Livestock farming has been seriously affected by the need to produce so much so quickly. Intensive battery farming is one result. Under present legislation, live animals are classified as 'agricultural products' — the same category as vegetables — to be used and abused with little consideration that they are living animals that feel pain just like us. Chickens, hens, pigs, cows and sheep have all had their lifespans dramatically reduced by the 'instant' farming methods of modern-day Britain.

The myth of happy and contented animals down on the farm is now far from the truth. Many of these creatures undergo intolerably cruel conditions which are ignored by the consumer and justified by the farmer. Natural immunity to disease is lowered as animals are pumped full of antibiotics; they are kept in cramped spaces often unable to turn around; they are not provided with straw to lie on; and they never see daylight. The life of a battery animal is highly stressed and completely unnatural.

Ninety per cent of our eggs come from battery hens. Kept crowded together, five hens live in one cage measuring 18″ by 20″ for a whole year. The cage is made of wire mesh with a sloping floor, and the hens cannot do anything that comes naturally to them, such as stretch their wings, scratch around, dustbathe or perch. Often, the end of their beaks may be cut off to stop the hens pecking each other out of sheer boredom and neurosis. After a year of intensive laying, the hen will be worn out and will go to the slaughterhouse to be added to soup, paste and pet food. The natural life of a hen is seven years, at the oldest, while a battery hen may last two and a half years.

Many broiler chickens suffer a similar, sickening fate. Packed into a huge, windowless shed, flocks of 20,000-100,000 birds are reared for seven weeks and then slaughtered. The breeds chosen grow very fast and have structural problems. As a result, they spend much of their time sitting down in the thick layer of muck which can inflict burns to their hocks and breasts, and they may also develop ulcerated feet. As the birds grow, they have less and less space to move around in. Out of 500 million chickens reared annually like this, between 20 and 30 million die before they even reach the slaughter-house. A further 2.5 million die on the way to the slaughterhouse from shock, suffocation and injury. Turkeys spend between 12 to 24 weeks in similar conditions.

Pigs are intelligent, sensitive animals, yet they too are submitted to virtual imprisonment at the hand of battery farming. During pregnancy, sixty per cent of breeding sows are kept in narrow stalls, made of concrete or metal bars. The sows do not have enough room to turn round, or move more than one step forward and one step back, and are often tethered to the ground by a girth strap or an iron neck collar. They take no exercise and their appetite lessens; out of frustration they gnaw the bars of the stall.

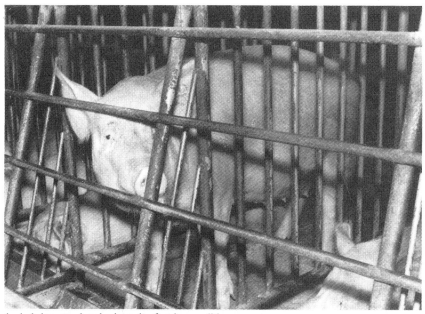

A pig being reared under intensive farming conditions.

When the time comes for farrowing, the sow is moved into another narrow crate where she will suckle her piglets for three weeks before they are taken to be fattened for bacon and pork. The sow's natural instinct is to build a nest of grass and leaves in which to give birth and rear her young, which she would then suckle for three months. Once the piglets are removed from the sow they are put in wire meshed cages decked on top of one another and, as soon as they are strong enough, are moved to concrete fattening pens, often with no straw for bedding. At four and a half months old, young pigs are taken for slaughter to be sold as pork; at six months old the remainder meet their end as bacon.

The average dairy cow produces 45-50 litres of milk every day, ten times the amount she would produce for a suckling calf. She is milked for 10 months of the year and pregnant for nine months. She is a frequent victim of mastitis (inflammation of the udder) and lameness. Despite the limitations of EEC milk quotas, several chemical companies are involved in bringing into commercial use the growth hormone — bovine somatotropin (BST). BST increases the milk yield of cows by 10 to 20 per cent. It has also been shown to increase mastitis and lameness and lower general condition.

The EEC has banned BST until further research has been completed. In the UK the National Farmers Union do not want BST, and neither do the public. In a recent NOP poll, 83 per cent of those questioned did not want to drink milk treated with BST. It appears that the only people that do want BST are the pharmaceutical companies who have genetically engineered the hormone and stand to make extra profits from its introduction.

Increasingly, sheep offal has been given to cows as a form of protein in their diet. This practice has coincided with the development of the cow disease bovine spongiform encephalopathy (BSE or 'mad cow disease') which is believed to affect one cow in every thousand. It is remarkably similar to a sheep disease known as 'scrapie', and a rare human disorder called Creutzfeldt-Jacob (CJ) disease, which culminates in senility. Unfortunately the BSE bug incubates for around three years, during which time the farmer is unaware of his cow's deteriorating health.

Campaigners are worried that infected milk could be sold on to the public and are also questioning whether there is a vicious circle in operation from sheep to cow to human. Whatever the results of investigation, it seems common sense to avoid feeding cows, which are ruminants anyway, with dead, possibly diseased sheep. The Government currently demands that cows diagnosed as having BSE are destroyed along with their milk.

Add to this the following facts:

★ Only one tenth of British slaughterhouses come up to EEC hygiene standards.
★ Live animals are transported across the continent packed tightly into lorries, often arriving half dead without having been fed or watered.
★ Ranchers are tearing down the rainforests to make hamburgers.
★ Around 40 per cent of cereals grown globally feed animals.
★ A fifth of the world's population is undernourished.
★ There are an estimated 0.38 hectares per person in the world and that a person on a Western diet needs 0.62 hectares.
★ Western intensive farming methods have brought untold problems to developing countries that should be growing crops of millet, sorghum and vegetables to feed their own people rather than exporting cotton, rice and maize to the Western world.
   ...and you can see that agriculture as a whole is in a pretty sorry state of affairs.

Organic farming

The picture painted is gloomy, but there is a very effective method of agriculture that is slowly gaining credence amongst farmers, government and consumers alike. Organic farming is described by its supporters as a sustainable policy for the future, and can be applied across the board: arable, dairy, beef, sheep, pig, poultry, vegetable and fruit. Organic farmers believe in putting back into the land what they take out, not starving it of nutrients and piling on the fertilisers. They believe in a humane rearing system for livestock, which is mindful of the needs of the animal in question, as well as the consumer. Organic farming means ethical farming.

There are over 1,000 organic farmers operating in Britain at the moment. On the continent there are 15,000. It takes between two and seven years to convert to a certifiable organic system and yields reduce by around 20 per cent after conversion. Farmers normally convert their farm bit by bit, in order to make ends meet until the conversion is complete. But once certified organic by the Soil Association, a farmer can charge a premium for produce to substitute the loss in yield.

A spread of organically-grown produce.

Organically farmed crops are not sprayed with any chemical pesticides and are not treated with nitrogen, potassium or phosphate fertilisers. Instead, farmers rely on manure, or green manure (crops that are grown and then ploughed back into the ground), one-off treatments of pyrethrum, sulphur or copper. Beneficial insects such as ladybirds, horseflies and lacewings are encouraged, not killed off, so that they eat up harmful aphids.

The most popular method or organic farming is using a multi-culture system in which crops are grown and livestock reared. On a typical multi-culture 100 acre farm, half of the land would be used for cropping and the other half for pasture. A typical use of one field would be as follows: for the first three years after conversion the field would be pasture, then three years of arable crops would be grown on it, such as wheat, barley and spring beans, then complete the rotation by turning the land over to pasture again. This ensures that the earth is enriched and is not overworked. Meanwhile, all the farmer's eggs are not in one basket and there is a much better mix of crops and livestock.

By converting land into pasture for several years, the land has a chance to recover and rid itself of the heavy level of chemicals in its soil. In the pasture (which is also known as a ley, ie. a temporary pasture) will grow lots of clover, chicory and deep rooted herbs. These plants bring nutrients up from the deeper soil and improve its structure making it very rich in trace minerals. This pasture land then is a very good source of food for grazing livestock, as well as the crops that will follow.

If animals are not included in the farm, then green manures, such as beans or peas, are used to form the nutrient base of the soil, rather than animal manure. But with either system, the same crops are not allowed to be sowed for more than one year in four so that any soil disease is not perpetuated. Cabbage, potatoes and onions are examples of crops that may leave diseases in the soil. If two crops of wheat were grown two years in a row, afterwards the land would undergo four years of pasture and then perhaps two years of vegetable crops.

The Soil Association, an independent regulating organic association, has set out standards for livestock husbandry which guarantees animals a decent life. In its newly launched Campaign for Safe Meat, it outlines the following standards:

— permanent housing of breeding stock is prohibited, therefore factory farming is out
— prolonged confinement or tethering of an animal is prohibited
— the size of herds or flocks should not be detrimental to the animals' behaviour patterns, ie. they should not be lonely or under severe stress
— all stock should have access to pasture during the grazing season
— organically grown feedstuffs form the basis of the animals' diet
— most additives and in-feed medication are prohibited
— treatment of healthy animals with unnecessary drugs is prohibited

There are far fewer organic farmers concentrating on livestock then there are on arable and vegetable crops. But there is a growing demand for organic dairy, meat and egg products. Three of the most successful organic concerns so far have been Welsh Organic Foods in Lampeter, West Wales Organic Growers and Brynllys Farm in Aberystwyth. Welsh Organic Foods make

Pencareg and Cardigan cheeses which are sold in several big supermarkets, and West Wales Organic Growers grow and pack a variety of vegetables.

Rachel's Dairy, part of the Brynllys Farm, produces cream, clotted and unclotted, wholemilk yoghurt, low fat yoghurt, butter, cottage cheese and buttermilk. All the milk used is taken from the Brynllys herd of 70 Guernsey cows, who also provide milk for Welsh Organic Foods for cheesemaking. In addition to the dairy, Brynllys grows cereals, vegetables and supports a flock of sheep. It is now open to the public as a prize example of how well organic farming can function.

A body of representative groups headed by the Soil Association believes that it is possible to turn 20 per cent of Britain's farming organic by the year 2000. The groups believe that the demand from consumers is increasing: in the first six months of 1989, sales of organic meat trebled, fruit and vegetable sales doubled and demand for organic cereals by millers quadrupled. Retailers are constantly unable to meet demand for organic produce and import around 60 per cent from abroad.

ORGANIC FOOD: growth and forecasts, 1987-2000			
	Organic Food £ million	All Household Food £ billion	% organic
2000	2500	49	5%
1996	1000	41	2.5%
1992	200	32.5	0.6%
1990	83	30.5	0.27%
1989	57	30.5	0.18%
1988	42	30	0.14%
1987	34	29	0.11%

Source: Projection 2000

The Soil Association, British Organic Farmers and the Organic Growers Association would like to see organic farming given the type of financial assistance that conventional farming receives from the Government. These groups believe that both the Set Aside and Beef Extensification schemes could go one step further and encourage organic farming. They would also like to see organic farms included in the Nature Conservancy Council's Environmentally Sensitive Areas (ESAs), to recognise the benefits organic farming brings to fauna and flora.

Many more farmers would be willing to undertake conversion if the Government were prepared to provide subsidies for the first five years to help re-equip. More training courses on organics at Agricultural Colleges should also be a priority, and grants should be available to the pioneering organic groups so that more research and support can be given to farmers. So far, these organisations have been independently funded.

Mixed arable and dairy farms and vegetable farms are the easiest to convert to organic: the huge arable farms of East Anglia are more difficult because of intense production systems, as are chicken and pig farms where only a minimum of land is owned and would not be large enough to accommodate free range farming. Models have shown that, with a 20 per cent conversion across Britain, cereal production would decrease by six per cent, oil seed rape by 12 per cent and milk by four per cent — not an enormous reduction when you consider the already existing and wasted surpluses.

The EEC has put together a directive to monitor organic production in Europe and to provide a definition of quality produce. The UK Government has launched UKROFS (the United Kingdom Register of Organic Food Standards), a voluntary register that offers certification and inspection services. However the Soil Association still remains the pioneering group which will continue actively to promote the benefits of organic farming to the unconverted.

The two best-known organic symbols — Ukrofs and the Soil Association.

Organic farming is not a nostalgic return to the good old days. It is simply a system that combines proven practices for healthy soil with the best in modern biological knowledge, and one that recognises animals as living creatures rather than inanimate objects. Organic campaigners look forward to the day when organic farming provides most of our food, and surely this is the best prospect for agricultural policy as it moves into the next century. The exploitation of land and animals has gone on far too long — after fifty years of experimentation, let's move on to better things.

Take Action

You

— turn your own garden organic, stop using nitrogen, potassium and phosphate fertilisers. Turn instead to compost, seaweed and manure. Avoid spraying your plants with pesticides, grow plants that encourage beneficial insects such as carrots, parsley, parsnips and nettles. For a plague, use one-off treatments of pyrethrum, deris, sulphur and copper formula
— buy organic fruit, vegetables, cereal products, meat, dairy produce and free range poultry and eggs as often as possible. Most larger supermarkets now stock organic fruit and veg, and a list of farm shops and organic butchers can be obtained from the Soil Association, 86 Colston Street, Bristol BS1 5BB

The Government

— set up a subsidy programme for farmers that want to convert to organic methods
— plough financial support into the research and development of organic farming. The independently funded Elm Farm Research Centre is the only advice and research centre open at the moment
— crack down on inhumane rearing of livestock, particularly poultry, pigs and dairy herds. Many Government and independent committees have already condemned factory farming
— encourage organic farming as a way to reduce massive European surpluses through Set Aside and Beef Extensification schemes.

Chapter 11

Food

Food is a necessity of life. It is essential to our health, happiness and well-being. Food also provides pleasure and social interaction; it dominates world economies and political systems. And, last but not least, its growth and production has a huge impact on the environment we live in.

Through all stages of food production, the environment comes into question: where food is grown or reared, how it is harvested or slaughtered, its processing, packaging and transportation, where it is sold; all determine the quality of the world we live in — our air, our water, our soil, our nourishment and our health.

As with many other issues, the 1940s marked a turning point in food production. Since the last World War, food in Britain has undergone a remarkable revolution — new foods, new processes, new substitutes for food, new markets, new means of transportation. The humble Sunday roast, or Friday's fish and chips, are becoming meals of the past as food technology is recognised as big business. With it has come greater variety and choice, as well as convenience and speed cooking. And, like any other revolution, there have been advantages and disadvantages for the unsuspecting and often vulnerable consumer.

The growth in knowledge of organic chemistry after the Second World War and the subsequent introduction of chemical nitrates, pesticides and hormones to promote intensive farming both of land and livestock has led to immense environmental difficulties. Depletion of the soil, pesticide and nitrate residues in water and food, coupled with inhumane methods of rearing animals in confined spaces, have been dealt with in Chapter 10.

But these are not the only areas of the agriculture and food industry which give rise for concern. Chemicals which pollute the environment and our bodies are introduced into many of the other processes through which food travels on its way from the farm to our shop shelves. Most people today live in towns or cities and hence rarely buy food which is 'fresh from the farm'. Most of it is preserved in some way; it is transported and various methods are employed to change and enhance its appearance; it may be prepared or pre-cooked for convenience and finally aesthetically packaged for maximum appeal.

Some of these methods are extremely useful. They ensure we have nutritious and appealing food all year round. Others are superfluous and, while enhancing the appeal of food, may lessen its nutritional value and increase its price. They may even introduce elements into the food which are detrimental to health and/or encourage pollution of the environment.

Preservation

Gone are the days when fruit and vegetables were eaten only in the area and season in which they were harvested, and a few put aside for home pickling or preserving. Today, fruit and vegetables are available every month of the year, if we are willing to pay the price of importing and employing the latest methods of food preservation.

Canning, freezing, drying, irradiation and the addition of preservatives, both natural and chemical, are just some of the methods available today to ensure availability of food. Each method has its advantages and disadvantages both to health and the preservation of the planet.

Firstly, the large-scale transportation of food comes up against environmental difficulties. While it may be very pleasant to eat strawberries in December, it is perhaps worth remembering the energy used to transport these luxuries from abroad, the extra fungicides and pesticides used to ensure that during the journey they do not deteriorate, and the fact that though the strawberries may appear fresh, they have probably been shipped thousands of miles and kept in cold storage for months. Such delays will reduce their food value resulting in the loss of vitamins and minerals.

Freezing food is kinder to the environment and to our health, for it destroys fewer vitamins and does not require chemical additives. However, frozen food does not retain the vitamins of fresh produce and the danger is to opt for frozen even if fresh food is available and hence miss out on valuable nutrients. A number of specialists in diet and health maintain that, for optimum nutrition, it is essential to eat 'live' food, that is fruit and vegetables in a raw state which has not been cooked, frozen or preserved.

Neither does canned food provide an environmentally friendly option for preserving food. Cans are made of valuable raw materials — aluminium, steel and tin which are rarely recycled. Moreover, cans are often soldered with a lead compound which could over the years be hazardous to health.

One of the problems of today's eating habits is that people expect food to last over longer periods. Our lifestyles dictate that a weekly shop at the local supermarket will suffice, and therefore supplies must last until the next excursion. This has encouraged manufacturers to doctor products with additives to preserve their shelf life. As such, some additives play a very useful role in slowing down the growth of micro-organisms and preventing the deterioration of fats and protein. However, in many cases they are not entirely necessary, and their use replaces more stringent hygiene procedures. Consumer pressure is now being put upon the food industry to cut down on such doctoring of foods and, at the same time, to provide quality durable produce.

While consumer demand is for 'natural' and 'additive-free' products, manufacturers have to seek out ways of making food last as long as possible, so irradiation is being promoted as a more viable alternative for prolonging shelf life in the future. By this method, produce is subjected to waves and particles generated by a radioactive source which kills off all living organisms, including bacteria, as well as delaying the ripening and decay of fruits and vegetables. The method is not yet permitted in the UK, but its practice on a limited basis is carried out in some 30 other countries in the world, and its introduction here is under discussion.

The World Health Organisation, the Food Agricultural Organisation of the United Nations and the Joint Expert Committee of the International Atomic Energy Agency all agree that food irradiation poses no risks to human health. But its uptake has not been popularly received in Britain. While it is clear that food treated with irradiation is not radioactive, ie. the rays cannot be passed from the food to the consumer, there is still uncertainty about whether such treatment leaves other dangerous chemicals in the food. Although irradiation does destroy all bacteria, it is not certain whether or not it removes the toxins that such bacteria may have released into the food, which could, after all, be the cause of food poisoning. Further concern rests with the nutritional value of the food after irradiation, in particular vitamin content, and lastly, there is the fear that irradiation will offer manufacturers the opportunity to sell second-rate produce in disguise.

Irradiation of food does not conform to attempts to cut down the number and scale of radiation emitters in order to reduce the risks of contamination of plant workers and local communities. Moreover, it could increase problems of disposal of radioactive waste.

Creating an image

Methods of preservation are just some of the ways our food is tampered with, be it to our loss or benefit. Far greater research and time is put into enhancing the taste and aesthetic appeal of today's food, and it is here perhaps that the most concern lies.

For some years, consumers have been aware of the dangers of additives in foods. In 1984 the EEC demanded proper labelling and this, along with publicity given to cases of additive poisoning and allergic reactions, has encouraged manufacturers to reduce their use. Despite the consumer alert, additives are still on the increase. At the beginning of the century, around 50 were used for a small number of functions. Today 3,800 are on the market used for over 100 functions.

Most are employed simply to enhance product appeal: colour, smell, texture or flavour. Others make products easier to process. Just as irradiation has the potential to mislead the consumer about the quality of food on sale, so the use of cosmetic additives can dupe customers about the nutritional value of the food they are buying. Additives can be used to enhance the appearance of poor quality food, for example polyphosphates which bind excess water into ham or fish, increasing the volume of the product yet diluting its nutrients. They may also serve to imitate foodstuffs such as meat or cheese.

Apart from a few, most additives have no nutritional value whatsoever. Some are even thought to be dangerous. Many of the flavourings which enhance our food today have not been thoroughly tested, or if they have, the testing has been done in isolation without taking into account the reaction it may have when combined with others. The London Food Commission in its research into 299 permitted additives, discovered that in 25 cases evidence existed of severe toxic hazard. Work carried out by allergy specialists has proved that there is now no doubt that ill-health can result when such additives are consumed; fits and hyperactivity in children is one of the most common complaints; workers in food factories processing additives have also been known to suffer, common ailments being respiratory problems and skin diseases.

The cost of processing and distributing food in the UK came to £17,381 million in 1984, which is more than half the total food bill, according to a study carried out by the London Food Commission. The discovery of colourants, flavour enhancers and emulsifiers has unfortunately meant that processed and ready made food can contain ingredients of substandard quality and nutritional value. Sadly, the methods used in food processing to boost flavour and enhance colour and texture are all too often detrimental to the nutritional value of the product: natural vitamins, minerals and fibre may be removed, and salt, sugar and cheap fats are introduced, all of which contribute to the already high levels of heart disease prevalent in this country.

Packaging

It's not only what's in the food that affects flavour, colour and general appeal, but also what the food is packaged in. Paper, foil, cling film and cardboard are just some of the wrappings which envelop and protect our food, particularly that which is processed. Most are there for aesthetic value in an attempt to raise the product's perceived value. While bumping up the price of our shopping bill, this only adds to the general burden of waste disposal (see Chapter 7). In addition, some packaging which comes into close contact with food has implications on human health and quality of food.

Most of the food we buy has at least one layer of plastic incorporated in its packaging. Because it does not biodegrade, plastic is a menace to the environment — it can also be undesirable from a human health point of view. Cling film wrapping, generally in very close contact with food, is now known to release plasticisers, potential carcinogens, into its contents. This occurs particularly with fatty foods, ie. cheese or meat. Film wrapping is now available without plasticisers, with the label 'non PVC' or 'contains no plasticisers' but, because of the disposal problem such packaging presents, it is better to avoid it altogether if possible.

Aluminium foil also comes under attack for health and environmental reasons. Some say cooking in aluminium foil presents a risk of the metal depositing in the food, not a pleasant prospect in view of the evidence of aluminium poisoning resulting in premature senility or Alzheimer's Disease. Apart from this risk to human health, aluminium foil takes a huge amount of energy to produce and is not an environmentally acceptable packaging.

A more recent concern is the risk posed by food which comes into close contact with bleached paper products. Evidence from Sweden, one of Europe's biggest paper manufacturing countries, states that the chlorine used in paper bleaching processes results in by-products known as dioxins, some of the most toxic substances known to mankind, which can migrate into food. Dioxins are known to cause cancer and to affect the immune and reproductive system of animals. Britain's Department of the Environment claims that the risk to humans is far smaller, 'human beings are much less sensitive to dioxins than many other species,' says its report on the subject. Nonetheless, evidence has shown disturbingly high contents of dioxins in humans.

> *Our bodies and the environment have levels of dioxins way above safety limits. There is no room for complacency, we need to act immediately to reduce the levels of this highly toxic chemical in our bodies.*
> Women's Environmental Network

Recent studies from the Ministry of Agriculture Fisheries and Food (MAFF) have now seen evidence of the migration of dioxins from chlorine bleached milk cartons into milk after a period of storage. Dioxins are also suspected to migrate into drinks made with chlorine-bleached coffee filter papers and tea bags, although MAFF states that the amounts extracted are very low and do not present a significant danger.

The extent of the risk to human health posed by the migration of dioxins into food is a controversial one, and it questions once again the extravagance of modern packaging methods at the expense of the environment and health. Chlorine bleached paper is no more hygienic than unbleached paper, but we have come to expect our packaging to be sparkling white rather than a dull grey or brown. As a result, the paper-producing countries of the world are now facing severe problems of ground and water contamination by dioxins. This poses a threat to agriculture and the food chain, and consequently to human health. Environmentalists claim that there is insufficient evidence to argue that dioxins are not harmful and therefore the precautionary principle should be enforced, and a ban be placed on all chlorine bleaching.

In Japan, Sweden and some other European countries, consumer pressure has made unbleached paper products available. Modifications in paper production technology have also reduced the use of chlorine.

Now it is up to the consumer to accept that white doesn't necessarily mean healthy and to opt for unbleached products. Better still, avoid paper altogether where possible; buy loose tea, and invest in a coffee percolator. Milk in returnable bottles is aesthetically pleasing, safer and a good deal more environmentally friendly than that in cartons.

Possible routes to Human Exposure from dioxins.

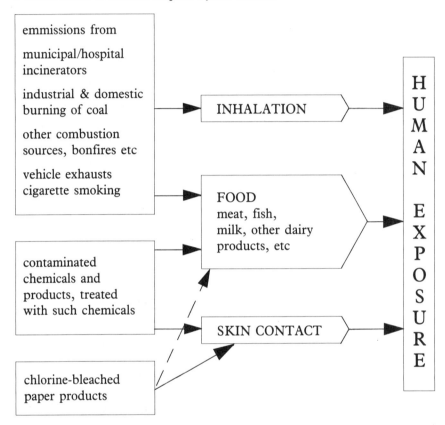

Source: Department of the Environment

Poison in our food

It would appear that, with the numerous methods of preserving food which abound in the Western World and the food industry's obsession for pristine packaging, food poisoning would be a thing of the past. But, despite many improvements in hygiene since the beginning of the century, 1988 saw the highest incidence of illness caused by contaminated food ever recorded.

Although there is no single cause for this, there is little doubt that our centralised system of mass food production, in particular of animal protein, has led to a situation where quantity has overridden quality, not just in terms of flavour and nutritional value, but also hygiene and human safety.

Salmonella is one of the most widely talked of hazards, and one which is most certainly on the increase: between 1983 and 1988, the number of reports by British laboratories of salmonella infection more than doubled. Because of the high incidence of salmonella enteriditis, a strain which resides in chickens, a link has been made between poultry farming methods and food poisoning.

Modern methods of livestock farming have come under severe attack since the 1989 outbreak of salmonella. Intensive rearing practices have been blamed, where animals kept in cramped and often unhygienic conditions are fed on high protein feeds often containing the remnants of slaughtered chickens contaminated with salmonella. The food is ingested and the bacteria may lie dormant in the bird, where it contaminates the eggs produced and can be excreted and spread around the flock.

The use of antibiotics in factory farming, both to combat infection and to promote growth, has also come under criticism in the salmonella scandal. Long-term use has led to the growth of resistant strains. Also, the methods practiced in today's abattoirs, where a conveyor-belt approach to the slaughter of animals is carried out at maximum speed, is often to the detriment of hygiene procedures.

Our increase in intensive farming has brought with it an increase in outbreaks of food poisoning. But it is not just farming methods which are to blame. Consumer reliance on processed and ready chilled foods has brought a new food poison to Britain: listeria. Although not a new phenomenon abroad, occurrences of listeria were relatively rare in Britain until 1989 when the number of cases rose to an estimated 800, one third of which were pregnant women. The unique and dangerous features of the listeria bacterium are that it appears to be transmitted through meat or even vegetables grown in areas fertilised by the manure of infected animals. Refrigeration, instead of killing the bacteria, encourages it. Consequently, listeria is found in chilled foods such as prepared salads and meats.

Another disturbing feature of the bacteria is its resistance to heat; cheeses, even those made from pasteurised milk, have been known to contain listeria. The prime victim, however, is the convenience supermarket meal which is cooked only to a certain temperature at processing stage, then chilled, trans-ported and briefly heated before eating. The heating is insufficient to kill the bacteria and the chilling encourages their growth. Dr Richard Lacey, pioneer of the research into listeria in this country, has revealed in his studies that out of nearly 100 cook-chill foods from supermarkets, nearly a quarter have been found to be contaminated with listeria.

The points outlined in this chapter demonstrate a theme which runs throughout this book: the increase in productivity, availability and consump-tion by the Western World is beginning to backfire. With the help of nitrate fertilisers, chemical pesticides, intensive livestock rearing and an array of artificial methods, we are able to produce food in excess. But at what cost? What about the state of our soil and our water, not to mention our own bodies polluted by chemicals and bacteria?

Protect yourself
— buy fresh, local and seasonal produce
— opt for organic fruit and vegetables, free range eggs and meat reared without antibiotics
— wash all fruit and vegetables thoroughly before use, peel where appropriate
— buy fresh rather than processed foods

Take Action
— avoid foods which are over-packaged
— write to your MP expressing your concerns
— write to your local supermarket expressing your desire to buy local unadulterated food
— join an environmental group to campaign on issues concerning pesticides and nitrates.

Chapter 12

Water

Once upon a time, anyone who stepped foot outside Britain would make a beeline for the nearest shop selling bottled water. Upset tums were the bane of foreign travel. Not so at home, where British tapwater had a reputation for its purity and safety. To lace an English dinner table with a bottle of French mineral water was considered an insult.

Just ten years on, sales of bottled water in Britain have reached an all time high of 175 million litres per year, a market worth £130 million. Water filters have become a popular household commodity, an indication of the public's concern or dissatisfaction with tapwater. But what has been the reason for this change in drinking habits? Are bottled waters just a passing fad, filters yet another trendy gadget for the kitchen, or has the quality of our water really changed?

Perhaps it is something to do with the fact that, until 1985, Britain had no specific standards to define the quality of drinking water. Consequently, no-one knew if what we were drinking was safe or not. A vague stipulation that drinking water should be 'wholesome', was all that emerged from the first and second Public Health Acts of the nineteenth century and the Water Act of 1973. It was not until 1980, when the EEC looked more closely at what was coming out of taps both on the continent and in Britain, that talk began to circulate about water standards. A Water Directive was issued covering some 60 different substances found in water, in particular toxins such as nitrates, pesticides, heavy metals and chemicals. It set guidelines of how much of each substance should safely be permitted in drinking water, and maximum admissible concentrations (MACs), levels which should not be exceeded.

EEC governments were given five years to meet the standards and to ensure their water did not exceed the MACs in any given sample. When the five year time limit drew to a close in 1985, it was revealed that some five million people in Britain were receiving sub-EEC standard water. Britain had made little effort to clean up supplies. To overcome its embarrassment the British Government granted exemptions for 350 British water sources, ie. it managed to stall implementation of the Directive on water sources containing levels in excess of EEC MACs of aluminium, nitrates, pesticides and iron, among others. The Department of the Environment also applied for a four-year delay on the implementation of lead parameters.

Rubbish gathered near the bank of the River Thames, London.

In 1989 Friends of the Earth released a survey showing how Britain's water fared nine years after the EEC Water Directive was issued. It reported that a large proportion of British water supplies continue to exceed the maximum admissible concentration levels laid down for nitrates, pesticides, lead, aluminium, and industrial chemicals. It appears Britain has made little or no attempt to reach EEC standards. Moreover, in July 1989 the House of Commons rejected a provision to be included in the water privatisation legislation proposed by the House of Lords which would have committed it to bringing drinking water up to EEC standards by 1993.

Nitrates

One major area of concern for water which does not reach EEC levels is the content of nitrates which it contains. Although nitrates are naturally present in small quantities in organic substances, heavy use of nitrate fertilisers on arable land — 3 million tonnes in the UK every year — gives cause for concern. Approximately half of the nitrate fertiliser put on the soil is taken up by crops, the other half remains in the soil and, being highly water soluble, seeps through into the underground aquifers, which supply water to 30 per cent of the nation.

The process is a slow one, which perhaps explains why action to stop the process has been delayed. The nitrates in the water we are drinking were probably put on the land some 30 years ago and have been gradually seeping into the water supply ever since. As the levels of nitrate used on arable land have risen since then, in 30 years time we can expect water to be even more contaminated by nitrates than it is now.

In 1980 the EEC Directive set guidelines of 25 milligrams of nitrate per litre. Maximum admissible concentrations were set at 50 milligrams per litre. The Friends of the Earth survey revealed that 74 water supplies serving more than one and a half million people in Britain contained levels of nitrate higher than those permitted by the EEC Directive.

Health authorities agree that water containing such levels of nitrate can cause mortality in infants from a disease called methaemoglobinaemia, or blue baby syndrome, whereby the infant's ability to carry oxygen is diminished and it suffocates. Nitrates also pose a potential risk for adults; studies on animals show evidence of stomach and oesophageal cancer formation as a result of nitrate reaction on the gut.

Pesticides

The vast amounts of toxic chemicals used each year to kill insects and weeds are another of the main reasons why British water supplies fail to meet European standards. Most pesticides are toxic to humans in very small doses causing symptoms such as nausea, giddiness, restricted breathing and even loss of consciousness. More chronic effects are the long-term influences which include cancer tumour formation, birth defects, allergies, psychological disturbance and damage to the immune system.

In 1987, the British Geological Survey (BGS) published a report stating that the pollution of groundwater by pesticides constituted a serious and growing threat to drinking water in Britain. In particular, it cited areas of East Anglia where intense arable farming on light sandy soils made an ideal combination for the easy leaching of pesticides into underground wells. Once in the groundwater, pesticides become much more mobile and persistent than in standard agricultural soil, said the BGS.

The more recent Friends of the Earth survey tells us that water containing levels of pesticide above the EEC's maximum admissible concentrations are common in London, the Home Counties, East Anglia and the East Midlands.

> *Numerous groundwater supplies especially in eastern England have been found to exceed the (admittedly very low and non specific) EEC guideline value for permissable concentration of total pesticides in drinking water.*
> British Geological Survey, 1987

The Department of the Environment has requested a relaxation of the maximum admissible concentrations of pesticides in drinking water. Its request has not been backed up by the medical establishment. The World Health Organisation claims that knowledge of the health effects of pesticides is still limited, in particular when a number of different types are mixed together haphazardly. Its recommendation is that the precautionary principle should be adopted.

Metals

Heavy metals in drinking water are also a problematic area for a government attempting to abide by European law. Lead, known for its damaging effects on children's development and the unborn foetus, is present in alarming quantities in our water. The main source is from lead piping which deteriorates and is absorbed by some types of water. It gets into the blood stream and ends up poisoning organs before lodging in the bones. In 1980 the Department of the Environment balked at a figure of £2 billion, the cost of removing lead piping from British homes. Instead it opted to treat water with further chemicals to prevent lead absorption.

The EEC Directive sets a limit of 100 micrograms of lead per litre. The Friends of the Earth survey claimed that, in the two years previous to its survey, more than 100 councils in England and Wales breached the Maximum Admissible Concentrations at some time.

> *In Scotland, the water is extremely soft, has a low pH and lead plumbing and lead lined storage tanks are extremely common. As a result it has been estimated that in over 10 per cent of houses in Scotland the first draw water contains more than 300 ug of lead per litre.* (ie. six times the EEC maximum admissable concentration)
> World Health Organisation, 1984

Another metal present in water which causes concern is aluminium. Sometimes found naturally in low levels of peaty waters, aluminium is more commonly added to water in the form of aluminium sulphate to remove particles in water which may discolour it.

A survey published in *The Lancet* by the Medical Research Council in January 1989 expressed concern at the constant exposure to aluminium in drinking water which it claimed had a link with Alzheimer's disease, or premature senility. The study looked at 80 districts in England and Wales and found that the risk of Alzheimer's disease was 1.5 times higher in districts where the mean aluminium concentrations exceeded 110 micrograms per litre, as compared to areas of only 10 micrograms per litre. At present the EEC MAC for aluminium is 200 micrograms per litre, well over the danger limit expressed by the Medical Research Council. Since the report, Thames Water and Wessex Water have made efforts to phase out aluminium in water treatment, proving that there are alternative treatments available. According to Friends of the Earth, some 154 councils in Britain have breached the EEC MAC for aluminium in the last two years.

Chlorine

Most people living in cities will be aware of an odour, if not a taste, of chlorine when drinking water from the tap. Adding chlorine to water is one of the most common methods used to destroy bacteria, and, while there is no doubt that water must be clean, there are fears that chlorine may be posing yet another hazard to health.

The problem with chlorine is that it combines with the natural acids found in water coming from peaty and moorland areas to form chloroform, a toxic compound known under the generic name of trihalomethanes (THM). Chloroform is suspected to being one of the causes of cancers of the bladder, rectum and colon.

The EEC has set a limit of 100 micrograms of THMs per litre. West Germany has opted for an even lower level — 25 micrograms. Meanwhile in England and Wales taps spewing out water with more than 100 micrograms per litre are widespread. 'You could travel across the Midlands from Montgomery to Lincoln without ever being sure of finding tapwater that did not exceed the limit', said a report in *The Observer* in August 1989.

What can be done?

It is the culmination of these findings over the last ten years which has convinced the British public that tapwater is not to be trusted. Hence the arrival of a multi-million pound bottled water industry and over 41 manufacturers each selling a range of water filters. But is this the answer? Bottled water is expensive and, according to a *Which* survey (Feb 89), cannot make claims to be any safer than tapwater, although some claim low nitrate levels. Water filters provide some reassurance in that they remove heavy metals disposing of the lead problem, take the chlorine out of the water and improve the taste. Several brands even claim to remove nitrates. But the disadvantage with some filtered water is that the beneficial minerals, such as calcium, copper and zinc are removed, as well as toxic ones.

Pressure from the EEC, concrete evidence from environmental groups showing the pollution of our water, and concern from the public have meant that the time has come for a massive clean up. With it comes one of the most controversial sell-outs of the decade — the privatisation of the water authorities.

Detergent pollution, Portpatrick, Dumfries & Galloway.

While EEC law will be just as severe with a privatised industry as a public one, environmentalists fear that the sell-out provides no adequate means of monitoring tapwater. The National Rivers Authority (NRA), a public body with responsibility for providing pollution control, water resource planning, flood protection and environmental conservation, has been established, but there has been no appointment of a similar watchdog for sewage and treatment works.

Consequently it is up to the consumer to take adequate steps to check drinking water quality. The Government has told water suppliers that they must provide consumers with information about tapwater quality, so you can demand an analysis of your tapwater from the local water authority and find out if it is in breach of EEC law. If it is, you can then complain to the European Commission of failure to comply with community law. (Write to Friends of the Earth for further details.)

An analysis from the water authority will not, however, give accurate information on lead content, as this is often deposited in water on its way to you through the pipes. If you fear you have lead pipes in your home, you should ensure water is allowed to run off for several minutes before drinking it. You can also apply for a grant form your local authority to replace lead piping with a safer metal.

As the water industry makes moves to comply with EEC standards, it seems inevitable that water prices will rise. This should mean safer, cleaner water for all, and will also mean a change in attitude: what was once considered a free commodity will now become a valuable asset, but one whose quality and cleanliness must always be carefully monitored and preserved.

Take Action
— consult your water authority for an analysis of your tapwater
— write to the EEC and your MP if your water does not come up to standard (see Friends of the Earth for further details)
— opt for organic produce to reduce pesticide and nitrate contamination of water.

Chapter 13

The Home

Issues such as the destruction of the ozone layer, acid rain and global warming are difficult to relate to back down on the Earth's surface, but the more research that is carried out, the more we become aware that it is ourselves, the inhabitants of the Earth, who are responsible for what happens to it. Our habits and lifestyles control the survival of the planet and ultimately our own healthy existence and wellbeing.

The more medical knowledge develops, the more aware we become of the causes of different illnesses. In the last 10 years a strong link has been established between a polluted environment and sick bodies. Between 1915 and 1980, four million new chemicals were recorded of which 60,000 were in common use, with around 1,000 being added every day.

Many of the products which we use every day in the home or at work, while temporarily improving our quality of life, act destructively on the environment. Toxic chemicals are not just released from industry, they flow out of our homes and workplaces every day of the week, polluting water supplies, fouling the air, destroying the stratosphere. Some are also suspected to be cancer-forming or mutagenic (causing defects in unborn babies). Others affect the respiratory tract or the skin or set up allergic reactions.

In the last fifty years, our lifestyles have changed dramatically. Consumerism has boomed since the 1950s, and with soaring spending has come a convenient and comfortable lifestyle — beautifully decorated and furnished homes, with kitchens equipped with the latest time-saving gadgets and powerful chemicals to ease the burden of housework. All are taking their toll on the environment and on our health. In this chapter we are not suggesting a return to the bare necessities of our grandmothers, nor a 'sack and sandal' approach to life. Consumerism is here to stay, but it is up to each and every one of us to be aware of products which are harmful both to the environment and to health (the two are inevitably linked), avoid them and seek out safe and environmentally friendly alternatives.

Wood treatments

Let's start with house buying. Unless you are buying a brand new building, you may have to 'protect' your home from infestation by insects, rot and damp before the building society will grant you a mortgage. To do this you will be offered wood preservatives, powerful pesticides chosen for their ability to kill insects and fungi and for their persistence — their ability to remain toxic for a long time. These magic potions are sprayed on floorboards, joists and timber lofts by professionals who subsequently supply a guarantee that your building is protected for x years. The problem is that these chemicals are not only poisonous to insects and fungi, but to animals and humans as well. The London Hazards Centre, an independent advice and information body, has produced a report on the risks to human health of such toxic treatments. It cites examples of individuals who have suffered long-term illnesses leading to epileptic fits and even death. Since publishing its report, the London Hazards Centre has heard of over 230 cases where individuals or groups have become ill after wood preservative treatments of homes and workplaces, or after exposure to the chemicals or treated wood in pre-treatment plants, timber yards and building sites.

> *Chemicals which are not allowed on our fields may be sprayed freely in our homes and places of work. Three million houses have been treated already. Next year at least half a million people including children, babies and the yet unborn, will receive what for many will be the biggest pesticide dose of their lives.*
> London Hazards Centre, November, 1988

It is not really surprising that people suffer adverse reactions from these chemicals when we look at the effects. Lindane, used in hundreds of DIY and professional wood treatments, is known to be lethal to humans in doses of around 3 grams. It can poison through the skin, acting as an irritant or allergen; it is known to cause epilepsy and can do damage to the blood, brain and nervous system. Lindane is also known to cause cancer in animals. Its use is banned in Japan, the USA and other countries.

Then there is Pentachlorophenol (PCP), another common chemical found in many DIY wood treatments. PCP is favoured for its preservative properties as a fungicide. In 1988 the United Nations Environmental Programme stated that the domestic use of PCPs was of 'particular concern because of the possible health hazards associated with the indoor application of wood preservatives'. It is banned in many countries and restricted to outdoor use only in the USA. Wood, air, dust and objects in buildings treated by PCP remain toxic for at least five years. It is highly poisonous, and has been known to cause around 1,000 deaths worldwide as well as numerous cases of nerve damage, paralysis, liver, kidney and heart disease.

These are just two of a number of dangerous chemicals which are used in remedial treatments of over 150,000 homes a year. Not to mention the number of private DIY applications being carried out. But are these treatments really necessary? And how effective are they? They haven't been around forever. Did houses crumble and fall before their adoption?

While the wood preserving and chemical industries are clear in their defence of chemical wood treatments, saying they are essential and safe, some timber firms believe too much emphasis is put on chemical solutions to timber pests. Even cheap woods should be naturally durable for at least five years or longer, providing they are kept dry. Moreover, using wood treatments is, say some architects, treating the symptoms not the cause. It is also questionable just how long the treatments do protect the wood, as they are often unable to penetrate far enough to be of long-term use. The chemicals which have been used already to treat three million of Britain's 22 million homes are still pouring out pollution into the environment. These pesticides are everywhere in the air, water, soil and in our bodies. Perhaps its time to look for different ways of protecting our homes.

Alternative methods

The best way to naturally protect a building from rot or fungi is to keep it dry. Central heating will do this and will also deter some insects. Safer treatments include those based on borax, soda (sodium carbonate), potash, linseed oil and beeswax. Painting timber with natural resin, oil stain varnishes and paint will help. If you must use toxic products, move out until all vapours have dispersed, keep windows open and cover treated wood with impermeable varnish.

Some firms are providing alternative wood treatments, that is not to say they are entirely safe, but they have been approved by the Nature Conservancy Council as being safe to use in areas where bats roost and on this basis are thus safe to humans. They are based on permethrin or boron and are available from:

★ Remtox (Chemicals) Ltd, 22 First Avenue, Pensnett Estate, Kingswinford, West Midlands DY6 7PP, Telephone 0384 401414.
★ Rentokil will carry out a non-chemical method for treating fungal decay by cutting away all rotten timber, removing sources of damp and carefully monitoring moisture levels. It is more expensive than chemical treatment, and does not provide a 30 year guarantee.

Safe paints

Once bought and safely treated, your home needs decorating. As anyone who has spent much time in a freshly painted unventilated room will know, paint too has its unpleasant side-effects, leaving decorators groggy, often with a pounding headache. Paint does contain toxic chemicals, as well as heavy metals which are given off in a gas during application and while the paint in drying. Even after the paint has dried, toxic particles can also flake off and could constitute a danger for young children. Many glosses, primers and varnishes traditionally used lead as a drying agent. Lead is known to have a damaging effect on young children's development and can harm the growing foetus. Such facts have led manufacturers to considerably reduce the lead content of their paints. However, it is not always easy to know by reading the label. Some of the lead free brands are:

★ Liquid glosses: B&Q Liquid Gloss, Crown Plus Two Liquid Gloss, Habitat Gloss, Jonelle Gloss Finish and Tesco Liquid Gloss.
★ Non drip glosses: B&Q Non-Drip Gloss, Crown Plus Two Non-Drip Gloss, Dulux Non-Drip Gloss, Home Charm Non-Drip Gloss, Marley Non-Drip Gloss and Tesco Non-Drip Gloss
★ Emulsion paint does not contain lead.

The best part of moving into a new home or doing up an old one is the finishing touches — furniture and fabrics. Here, there is a multitude of choice and again environmental and health factors must be taken into consideration. If you opt for wooden furniture, be it kitchen fittings or stripped pine doors, you must take into account where the wood is coming from. Does it originate from a sustainable source or is its production resulting in the loss of valuable homes, land and habitat?

This does not mean you have to abandon your dream wood fitted kitchen. There are alternative sources of wood: Britain now imports temperate woods from sustainably managed sources (where trees are immediately planted to replace those which are cut down). These woods include oak, ash, beech, pine, alder, pear and apple wood and generally come from Canada, USA and Europe. Some of the products will be stamped with the *Good Wood Guide* Seal of Approval.

Energy efficient
Another major issue on environmental agendas is energy, described in detail in Chapter 2. What goes into our homes, the type of heating we choose, how much hot water we use and the number and variety of electrical appliances we possess, is crucial to global issues, since the more energy and resources we expend, the more emissions we release into the atmosphere and the more we contribute to pollution of the atmosphere.

Figures for sales of washing machines, tumble dryers and dishwashers have grown ten-fold since the end of the 1950s. This means more energy and water are used and more detergent is pumped into our waterways. But this is not a plea to return to the days of scrubbing and pounding by hand. Some manufacturers, aware of the pressure we are putting on our planet, have come up with machines which will run on nearly 50 per cent less water than traditional machines, 44 per cent less detergent and nearly 30 per cent less electricity. These are some of the recommended buys.

WASHING MACHINES
★ Zanussi Jetsystem FJ1011/FJ1023/FJ1015; washer and turbo dryer WDJ1013/WDJ1015.
★ AEG Lavamat Sensotronic 720/770/981
★ Bendix Autowasher 800 71668/71968

★ Hoover Logic 1300
★ Electrolux WH 1125
★ Hotpoint Electronic 9520
★ Candy Turbomatic 38 WD

DISHWASHERS
★ Zanussi TCR DW66TCR/DS20TCR/DS15TR
★ AEG Favorite 865/667/535
★ Candy Sylenma 650
★ Creda Debonair Super Deluxe 17901
★ Philips ADGG 664
★ Servis 4145

The use of fridges and freezers poses yet another environmental hazard — CFCs. The more fridges that are made, the more old models are casually disposed of, the more CFCs are released into the atmosphere. The green rule with fridges is do not replace your fridge unless you really have to, and above all don't just dump it. Some retailers of fridges will safely dispose of your fridge if you buy your new one from them, but as yet there is no national scheme for the safe disposal of fridges.

> *The DOE should hold urgent consultation with both the CFC and refrigeration manufacturers to devise collection and recycling schemes for redundant appliances and consider what powers are needed to ensure that CFCs are not allowed to escape into the atmosphere from this source.*
> House of Commons Environmental Committee report, June, 1988

Meanwhile manufacturers are working at reducing the amounts of CFCs used in refrigerants and some have cut levels by 50 per cent, none can claim so far to be ozone friendly however.

'Turn the lights out!' is a cry most of us heard often as children. Now it is not just a question of saving the pennies, but saving the planet. More than 20 per cent of energy generated in the UK is used for lighting and approximately half is wasted on lights being left on in empty rooms or as heat produced by inefficient lamps. You can cut your bills and your energy consumption significantly by using fluorescent lighting or energy saving bulbs:

★ Wootan Dulux EL — a range of light bulbs designed to use less electricity, which can be interchanged with normal incandescent bulbs. They are more expensive to buy but savings are made on consumption of electricity.

Keeping clean

Once the basics have been established in your home it is necessary to keep it clean and sparkling. To do this, the local supermarket will supply you with a huge selection of whiteners and brighteners, scourers and sprays. The first green rule here is use the minimum, consider what you really need and stick to it. You may find one all-purpose cleaner which does most jobs in the house.

Soap and detergents contain phosphates which contribute to eutrophication of water.

The more detergents and bleaches we pour down our sinks the more we pollute our environment. Detergents contain petrochemicals which cannot be broken down in the rivers, phosphates which promote the growth of algae swamping out other plant and fish life, and perfumes, enzymes and colourants which poison the fish and animal life of the waterways. Again, with the growth in awareness of the environment, some manufacturers are producing detergents which are formulated using natural ingredients as far as possible, and can be broken down in a minimum time and therefore do not pose such a risk to the environment. They are available in health food stores and some supermarkets and include these brand names:

★ Ark
★ Ecover
★ Faith
★ Homecare
★ Janco
★ Nitor

Also look out for 'own brand' supermarket products. Another major polluter in household cleaning products are aerosol sprays which use CFCs to propel their contents into the air. Like the CFCs used in fridges, they destroy the ozone layer — our shield from the sun's harmful rays. Most manufacturers now realise the dangers CFCs present and are phasing them out of products. You can help by buying only aerosols with the 'ozone friendly' or 'CFC free' label. Even better, opt for pump action sprays which are less irritating to the lungs and nostrils and more economic.

Making your home environmentally friendly does not mean making it uncomfortable, unattractive or old-fashioned. As shown above there are alternatives to the pollutants spewed out into the environment from our homes which are equally efficient without presenting a risk to energy sources, food and water supplies and ultimately our own health. As consumers we have the power to demand that the goods on shop shelves are environmentally sound. The more we refuse the ones that are not, the less we shall see of them. Being green is no longer a step backwards, it is looking to new and safe products of the future.

Useful Addresses

In any correspondence, please include self-addressed stamped envelope.

General

Ark
498-500 Harrow Road
London
W9 3QA

Friends of the Earth
26-28 Underwood Street
London
N1 7JQ

Greenpeace
30-31 Islington Green
London
N1 8XE

World Wide Fund for Nature
Panda House
Weyside Park
Godalming
Surrey
GO7 1XR

World Health Organisation
1211 Geneva 27
Switzerland

Acid Rain

Acid Rain Information Centre
Department of Environment & Geography
Manchester Polytechnic
John Dalton Extension
Room E310
Chester Street
Manchester

The Swedish Secretariat on Acid Rain
The Environmental Council
80 York Way
London
N1 9AG

Agriculture

The Soil Association
86 Colston Street
Bristol
BS1 5BB

(The above address is also home to British Organic Farmers and The Organic Growers Association).

Compassion in World Farming
20 Lavant Street
Petersfield
Hampshire
GU32 3EW

Disappearing Countryside

Council for the Protection of Rural England
Warwick House
25/27 Buckingham Palace Road
London
SW1W OPP

Council for National Parks
45 Shelton Street
London
WC2H 9HJ

Countryside Commission
John Dower House
Crescent Place
Cheltenham
Gloucestershire
GL50 3RA

Endangered Species

The Whale and Dolphin Conservation Society
20 West Lea Road
Bath
Avon
BA1 3RL

The Environmental Investigation Agency
208-209 Upper Street
Islington
London
N1

The IUCN Conservation Monitoring Centre
219c Huntingdon Road
Cambridge
CB3 0DL

Energy

Association for the Conservation of Energy
9 Sherlock Mews
London
W1M 3RH

Centre for Alternative Technology
Llywyngwern Quarry
Machynlleth
Powys
Wales

Department of Energy
House C
Millbank
Westminster
London

Energy Technology Support Unit
Building 156
Harwell Lab
Didcot
Oxfordshire
OX11 ORA

Food

British Agrochemicals Association
4 Lincoln Road
Peterborough
Cambs
PE1 2RP

Environmental Medicine Foundation
Symondsbury House
Bridport
Dorset
DT3 6HB

Hyperactive Children's Support Group
59 Meadowside
Angmering
Littlehampton
Sussex
BN16 4BW

London Food Commission
88 Old Street
London
EC1V 9AR

Ministry of Agriculture Fisheries and Food
Whitehall Place
London
SW1A 2HH

Ozone Layer

United Nations Environmental Programme (UNEP)
c/o IIED
3 Endsleigh Street
London
WC1H ODD

Stratospheric Ozone Review
Group (SORG)
Department of the Environment
2 Marsham Street
London
SW1

(Both SORG reports available from HMSO)

House of Commons Environment Committee
House of Commons
Westminster
London
SW1

Rainforests

Living Earth
10 Upper Grosvenor Street
London
W1X 9PA

Vehicles

Campaign for Lead Free Air
3 Endsleigh Street
London
WC1H 0DD

Transport 2000
Walkden House
Euston
London
NW1 2GJ

Waste

Waste and Recycling
Aluminium Federation
Broadway House
Calthorpe Road
Five Ways
Birmingham
B15 1TN

Association of Recycled Paper Suppliers
c/o Paperback Ltd
Bow Triangle Business Centre
Unit 2
Eleanor Street
London
E3 4NP

British Plastics Federation
5 Belgrave Square
London
SW1X 8PH

British Glass Manufacturers Confederation
Northumberland Road
Sheffield
S10 2UA

References and Further Reading

The Greenhouse Effect

The Heat Trap: The Threat Posed by Rising Levels of Greenhouse Gases, J Karas & P Kelly (Friends of the Earth, 1988).

The Greenhouse Effect: A Practical Guide to the World's Changing Climate, Steward Boyle & John Ardill (New English Library, 1987).

Energy

Friends of the Earth: Energy Without End, Michael Flood (Friends of the Earth Trust, 1986).

Efficiency of Energy Use (Friends of the Earth, 1989); *Electricity for Life,* Jim Skea (Friends of the Earth/CPRE, 1988).

Association for the Conservation of Energy.

Norweb: *Proposals for Renewable Energy in the Norweb Area,* (HMSO, 1989).

Centre for Alternative Technology.

Department of Energy: *Renewables, 1988 series* (Energy Technology Support Unit).

Acid Rain

The Swedish Environmental Protection Board: *Acidification and Air Pollution, Acid News* (Ingvar Bingman).

The World Wide Fund for Nature: *Acid Rain and Air Pollution,* Jacqueline Sawyer (WWF, 1989).

The Acid Rain Information Centre.

The Forestry Commission: *Forest Health Surveys 1987*, J L Innes & R C Boswell (HMSO, 1988).

Greenpeace: *Acid Waters*, Andrew Tickle (Greenpeace, 1988).

Wildlife Link: *Acid Rain and Wildlife* (Wildlife Link, 1988).

Air Pollution (HMSO, Department of the Environment, 1988).

The Ozone Layer

UK Stratospheric Ozone Review Group (SORG), *Stratospheric Ozone 1987* (HMSO, 1987); *Stratospheric Ozone 1988* (HMSO, 1988).

UNEP, *The Ozone Layer* (UNEP, 1987).

House of Commons Environment Committee, First Report, *Air Pollution Volume 1 (1987-88)* (HMSO, 1988).

Friends of the Earth: *The Montreal Protocol 1989*, Fiona Weir (Friends of the Earth, 1989); *Ozone Depletion 1988*, Fiona Weir (Friends of the Earth, 1988); *Alternatives to CFCs* (Friends of the Earth, 1989).

Vehicles and Transport

Transport and Atmospheric Pollution, Malcolm Ferguson (Earth Resources Research Ltd., 1989).

Getting There: A Transport Policy (Friends of the Earth, 1987).

The Campaign for Lead Free Air (CLEAR)

Rainforests

The Primary Source, Norman Myers (Norton, 1985)

Friends of the Earth: *Rainforest Briefing Pack, The Rainforest Times, The Good Wood Guide*

Living Earth: *Paradise Lost?* (Earthlife Foundation, 1986).

The World Wide Fund for Nature

Waste

Once is Not Enough: A Recycling Policy for Friends of the Earth, Alistair Hay (Friends of the Earth, 1989).

The Environment: The Government's Record (Friends of the Earth, 1989).

Toxic Pollution Briefing (Greenpeace, 1989).

Endangered Species

The World Wide Fund for Nature: Factsheets; *Biological Diversity — Saving the Wealth of Life on Earth; WWF News.*

Greenpeace: *Wildlife Briefing, Whales and Whaling.*

The Environmental Investigation Agency: The Trade in Live Wildlife Nick Carter & Dave Curry (EIA, 1987) *Injury, Damage to Health and Cruel Treatment* (Animal Welfare List & Humane Society of the USA, 1985).

The Whale and Dolphin Conservation Society: International Whale Bulletin No. 4 and No. 5, 1989.

The IUCN: *The 1988 Red List of Threatened Animals; Red Data Books on mammal, amphibia-reptilia, plant, invertebrate, fish, bird* (IUCN, 1988).

The Domesday Book of Animals, David Day (Ebury Press, 1981).

Disappearing Countryside

The Council for the Protection of Rural England: *Permitted Use Rights in the Countryside* (CPRE, 1989); *Welcome Homes* (CPRE, 1988); *Concrete Objections* (CPRE, 1988); *Superb Conversions,* Charles Watkins & Michael Winter (CPRE & Centre for Rural Studies, Royal Agricultural College, Cirencester, 1988); *Growing Against the Grain* (CPRE); *Paradise Protection, The Changing Face of England* (CPRE, 1989).

Transport 2000: *Transport Report,* July/August 1989

The Countryside Commission: *Planning for a Greener Countryside* (Countryside Commission, 1989).

Council for National Parks: *Tourist Complexes in National Parks,* Amanda Nobbs (CNP, 1988).

Department of the Environment: *Permitted Use Rights in the Countryside, The Future of Development Plans* (HMSO, 1989).

Farming and Agriculture

The Soil Association; British Organic Farmers; The Organic Growers' Association — *20% of Britain Organic by the Year 2000*, July 1988.

The Soil Association: *What is Organically Grown Food?*; *Nitrates in Food and Water*, Nigel Dudley (London Food Commission, 1986); *A Manifesto for Organic Agriculture*, Julian Rose & Nigel Dudley (Soil Association, 1987); *Campaign for Safe Meat*, Nigel Dudley, Mandy Pullen & Sue Stolton (Soil Association); *Drifting into Trouble*, Nigel Dudley (Soil Association, 1989); *The Case for Organic Agriculture*.

Compassion in World Farming

Food

Chemical Children, Dr Peter Mansfield & Dr Jean Monro (Century Paperbacks, 1987).

Food Adulteration and How to Beat It, The London Food Commission (Unwin Hyman, 1988).

Safe Shopping, Safe Cooking, Safe Eating, Dr Richard Lacey (Penguin, 1989).

Water

National Drinking Water Quality Survey, Friends of the Earth (*The Observer*, 1989).

International Agency for Research on Cancer (1987).

Biennial Report 1986-87 (World Health Organisation)

Which? February 1989/May 1989.

The Pollution Threat from Agricultural Pesticides and Industrial Solvents: A Comparative Review in Relation to British Aquifers, Hydrogeological Research (British Geological Survey 1989).

Hydrogeological Report 1987 (Natural Environmental Research Council).

The Home

Toxic Treatments, (London Hazards Centre Trust Ltd., 1989)

The Green Consumer Guide, Elkington & Hailes (Victor Gollancz, 1988)

Home Ecology, Karen Christensen (Arlington Books, 1989)

The Natural House Book, David Pearson (Conran Octopus Ltd, 1989)

Unless otherwise indicated, all photographs in this book are © Ecoscene.

Index

YOUR MONTHLY GUIDE TO HEALTHY LIVING

SUBSCRIBE TO *Here's Health*
AND GET TWO ISSUES FREE!

Enjoy a saving while you enjoy healthier living! Subscribe to **Here's Health** magazine and get 14 issues for the price of 12. What's more, wherever you live in the UK, you don't pay a penny for postage.

In each issue you'll get reliable guidance on the right foods, the right exercise, and the right lifestyle — and on natural methods of healing. You'll also be kept up to date on our "Clean Up Green Up" campaign to transform the face of Britain, a vital monthly report for everyone who wants to see our environment improved.

If you care about your health and your environment, you won't want to miss a single issue . . . so why not make sure of **Here's Health** every month by having it delivered straight to your door. Just call our Subscription Hotline on ☎ **0235 865656**, or complete and post the coupon below to: Here's Health, PO Box 35, Abingdon, Oxon OX14 4SF.

☎ **CREDIT CARD HOLDERS**
Order your Here's Health subscription
by phone. Simply dial
(0235) 865656
and quote your Access or Visa No.

Subscription Rates
UK: 14 issues for £12 (postage free). Overseas rates available on request.

Free postage if you live in the UK

☐ YES, please send me 14 issues of **Here's Health** for the price of 12.

☐ I enclose cheque/PO for £ _____ payable to Here's Health

OR

☐ Please charge £ _____ to my Visa/Access card

Name _____ (BLOCK CAPITALS)

Address _____

_____

Number

Expiry date _____ Signature _____ Post Code _____ Tel. _____

☐ Please tick here if you do not wish to receive details of any special offers or new products.

G290GG